Politics in the Purple Kingdom: The Derailment of Vatican II

George A. Schlichte, Ph.D.

With Editorial Assistance
by
Joan Stockbridge

Sheed & Ward

Sheed & Ward™ is a service of The National Catholic Reporter Publishing Company.

Library of Congress Cataloguing-in-Publication Data

Schlichte, George A., Ph.D.
    Politics in the purple kingdom : the derailment of Vatican II / George A. Schlichte : with editorial assistance by Joan Stockbridge.
      p.   cm.
  ISBN 1-55612-607-7 (alk. paper)
    1. Schlichte, George A., 1921- . 2. Ex-priests, Catholic--United States--Biography. 3. Catholic Church--Government--Controversial literature. 4. Vatican Council (2nd : 1962-1965) I. Title.
BX4668.3.S35A3 1993
282'.092--dc20
[B]   92-44098
                                         CIP

Published by: Sheed & Ward
               115 E. Armour Blvd. P.O. Box 419492
               Kansas City, MO 64141-6492

To order, call: (800) 333-7373

Contents

Acknowledgments v

Foreword vii

Introduction xii

  1. State of the Question 1

  2. The Magic of the Rules 2

  3. The Solace and Meaning in Rules 6

  4. Rules Structure Behavior 20

  5. Rules Applied 30

  6. Rule Master in the Purple Kingdom 40

  7. Life in the Purple Kingdom 45

  8. Rule Changes in the Air; John XXIII Elected Pope . . 60

  9. Archbishop Cushing, Complex Showman 65

10. The Inner Sanctum Plots Sabotage 76

11. Gale Force Winds of Rule Change 80

12. I Cross the Rubicon 89

13. Eye of the Storm 94

14. Victory in Rome 104

15. Scuttled by the Rules 111

16. The U.S. Naval Academy Shows the Way 119

17. The Man in the Arena 123

Glossary 124

Acknowledgments

Thanks to the help and encouragement of many, this work will see the light of day. I sincerely hope it contributes at least to a better understanding of the dynamics involved whenever an institution faces radical rule changes. Those involved will know their experiences are not unique, but integral to the nature of any organization.

This work began after my retirement from Blue Shield of Massachusetts in November 1988. My brother, Miles Schlichte, pointed out that I had lived through some extraordinary events and been privileged as few others to participate in the activities of very senior church officials. He urged me to write down my experiences, which I did. One of his daughters, Barbara Wierzbicki, characterized my first draft as a "brain dump." Her sister, Joan Stockbridge, came to my rescue, pointed out the emerging theme of goal displacement by the rules, did a chapter outline and sent me back to the word processor. When she heard of its imminent publication, she volunteered to edit the manuscript "for the sake of the family's reputation" and I am grateful to both of them.

Once the initial draft got revised, I imposed on two former Pope John Seminary faculty members. John Mahoney and Gerry Donovan both gave generously of their time and provided me with major reforms. Rita Rains found the theme and the story very much in accord with her own experiences. I wish to thank her for reinforcing my resolve to stay with the task of writing. John Mahoney evaluated the final draft as focused, with the story well told.

To pull the work together, Bud Robertson came to my side. He reviewed the work, chapter by chapter, and pointed out the disconnected sentences. He also did double duty as my Protestant reader who made me explain such foreign terms as "Monsignor."

One of my roommates at the Naval Academy, John Haynie, served on the administrative staff during rule changes there. He helped me learn how the Academy listened to the Board of Visitors and put me in touch with another classmate, George Grkovic, who served as the secretary of that Board during the time it developed the radical rule change recommendations. John Haynie also read a draft and said I had developed a best seller. I thank both of them.

With the manuscript in better shape, I turned to my neighbors. Harry Goff thought the material interesting, as did Sam Labate, who sent his comments to Sheed & Ward. Don Marcus encouraged pursuit of publication. He asked one of his friends, formerly in the publishing business, to review the manuscript. Back came the verdict of a marketable product. I am grateful to all these people for their encouragement.

Mario, Anne and Jeanne Umana have me in their debt for the title to the work, as well as for helpful clarifications. Jeanne helped especially with the Introduction, insisting that potential readers needed reasons to continue with the book.

Bonnie Baranowski struggled through an early draft. I thank her and appreciate her insistence that I define my reasons for writing the book.

Special thanks must go to a special reader, Lucy DiPrima, who takes care of my hair at Salon Forty-Four in Charlestown. Born and raised in St. Mary's parish, she read two drafts and gave both helpful comment and encouragement.

Meanwhile, I kept revising the text. Al and Charlotte Browne-Mayers kept after me to get to a publisher and were kind enough to read my revisions.

Enter Bill Alpert, pastor of the Unitarian/Universalist Church in Leominister, Massachusetts. He invited me on Palm Sunday to address his congregation as one of the speakers in his Living Prophet Series. My talk summarized the manuscript. It was well received. Bill asked if he could send a copy of it to Bill McSweeney, publisher of the *National Catholic Reporter*. The rest is history. NCR owns Sheed & Ward, whose editor-in-chief, Bob Heyer, called me to report their interest in publishing the *Purple Kingdom,* for which I am grateful.

Finally, I wish to thank Dick McBrien for his positive comments on the manuscript. I am grateful also to Bishop Mathews for his review of the manuscript and willingness to be quoted, as I am to Tex McClain and Charlotte Browne-Mayers.

George Schlichte
October 5, 1992

Foreword

One Saturday afternoon at Cape Cod, after we'd polished off some mussels and were waiting for blueberry pie to appear, my uncle, George Schlichte, handed me a draft manuscript of this book. After a quick perusal, I was hooked. The manuscript intrigued me with its inside stories of Rome, but, more importantly, I was compelled by its organizational analysis of the post-Vatican II Church. Now, two years later, after many conversations, consultations, and editing sessions I am writing this Foreword to provide a backdrop for the work that follows.

During my childhood, Uncle George was a near mythic figure. Many Sunday mornings my mother would announce, "Father George is going to say Mass at Grandparents' today." Hurrah! We wouldn't have to make a trek into our parish church and listen to the priest mumble an endless Mass, our knees and backs on fire as we knelt on thin plastic-backed kneelers. No, my brothers and sisters and I could walk with our parents up the hill to our grandparents' lovely, sun-flooded house where one of us would be chosen to take the traveling Mass kit out of the back closet. The Mass kit was a novelty from my uncle's days in Rome. About the size of a large jewel case, it was made of the finest kid leather and contained, among other treasures, a gold chalice and paten. The flat white wafers which would become the body of Christ were stacked in a marvelous sort of silver telescoping dish which no one, save my uncle, was allowed to open.

In front of the granite fireplace, Uncle George, resplendent in silk and gold embroidered vestments, would invoke the Divine and perform the sacred mysteries in front of our very eyes. His homilies, short and to the point, invariably addressed the behavior of nieces and nephews seated in a semicircle before him. No wonder that Father George, as we called him then, seemed the very embodiment of magic and mystery and authority.

Furthermore, my uncle's aura extended beyond the merely familial. Etched in my memory is the image of his hand extended in blessing as he sat on a stone garden bench, pink roses cascading on either side. A covey of Italian women in black dresses knelt before him, awaiting his benediction. The setting was the annual clambake of the large clan of a Sicilian family whose legal needs were tended to by my father. And as I frolicked around the garden, clad in one of four identical gingham dresses made by my mother, I heard the buzzing in all corners of the grounds. "The Monsignore!" Not only was my uncle a priest, he'd lived in Rome and spoke Italian like a native. I was swept to the head of the food line and served up an especially choice lobster and an enormous helping of steamed clams.

All this reflected glory came to an abrupt halt one summer morning in 1968 when I was 12 years old and woke to find the *Boston Globe* spread over the dining room table. I could read the headlines myself. "Rector Defies Pope. Says Paul VI Wrong about Birth Control." What could this mean? Surely my uncle could not be fighting with the Pope! I was stunned and frightened, my unease heightened by the tension that settled in at home, my mother and grandparents becoming glacial as my father championed the cause of his renegade brother. As it turned out, my personal experience was a youngster's microcosm of the dismay and confusion experienced by many Catholics in the period following the second Vatican Council.

George Schlichte's life provides a unique vehicle to examine the changing attitudes towards authority in the Roman Catholic Church. At the age of 25, having grown up in a traditional, rigorous Catholic home and served valiantly as an officer on the *USS Philadelphia* during World War II, he entered the seminary. Because of his wartime experience, he was called to Rome to finish his studies at the Gregorian University, the premiere institution for training priests worldwide. After spending less than two years in a parish, he returned to Rome and began his career as a member of the Roman Catholic bureaucracy. An unquestioning son of the church, he quickly rose through the ranks, becoming Business Manager and Vice Rector of the

North American College in Rome. From the outset, he was noted for his obedience to line authority. As one of his students observed, "If the Rector told him to take ten students outside and shoot them, his only question would be, 'Front door or back?'"

In 1964, after 15 years in Rome, George Schlichte was recalled to the Archdiocese of Boston, where, after two years of acting as Cardinal Cushing's vice chancellor, he started the Pope John XXIII National Seminary. At the seminary, he had a major personal awakening. Issues that had long remained dormant came to the surface. He remembered that after experiencing the horrors of war, he had entered the priesthood in an attempt to help people make sense out of life and to participate in the grand reconstruction of society. Suddenly, his role as Catholic rule enforcer seemed trivial and inconsequential. Simultaneously, he was exposed to the excitement of his faculty members who were aflame with the new theology endorsed by the Second Vatican Council. At dinner table tutorials, he was immersed in a heady academic atmosphere, fueled by debates over the nature of authority and the true role of the church. Old rules had been declared void: it was no longer a sin to eat meat on Friday. Previously unalterable rituals had been transformed: Mass was said in English; the altar was turned around so the priest could face the people. Mysterious points of dogma had been revised: Limbo no longer existed; indulgences were no longer a means of shortening time spent in Purgatory; as a matter of fact, Hell itself was redefined. No longer a place of eternal torment, Hell was seen as a situation one created by isolating oneself from the love of others and God. Furthermore, the Church no longer was seen as a strictly hierarchical, monarchical institution whose true purpose was to keep alive the line of authority stretching from Jesus and the apostles through to the Pope and bishops. No, the Church was the Servant of the People. Or perhaps it was a Sign of Grace. Regardless of the precise analysis, the fundamental point was that these topics were suddenly open to debate.

In this atmosphere, George Schlichte began to test his own assumptions. The archconservative became an advocate of the new theology. He began to run the seminary like a New England town meeting. Shared decision-making and concern for the needs of others became the operating principles, rather than authority and obedience. The chapel was packed each Sunday with laypeople from neighboring towns who were desperate to understand why the church they had grown up in had suddenly changed. Faculty members published papers, George Schlichte made statements to the newspapers and other media, newly-ordained graduates were assigned to preach and teach the new theology in parishes all over the world. Pope John XXIII Seminary had become a successful working experiment that promoted and applied the principles of Vatican II. Then, conservative members of the American and Roman hierarchy waged an intense campaign to remove George Schlichte as the rector of the seminary and to bring its faculty back into line with traditional teachings of the church.

After protracted infighting, including a recall to Rome for questioning, George Schlichte was pushed to resign. His political defeat can be seen as an example of the manner in which conservative Catholic authorities attempted to suppress the empowering vision of Vatican II. Furthermore, the victory of the traditionalists in shutting down the dissemination of the new theology can be viewed as a great loss for millions of confused Catholic faithful. Once the genie was out of the bottle and the physical reforms had begun to be implemented throughout the world, observant laypeople desperately needed information and support. A *New Yorker* cartoon reveals the dilemma. A horned, long-tailed devil leans on a pitchfork and asks his cohorts, "What do we do now with the ones in here for eating meat on Fridays?" While the cartoon humorously captures the essence of the dilemma, it also plays off of conflicting emotions some Catholics felt at the time. Many asked themselves whether they'd been overly naive and gullible, whether they'd foolishly left personal moral judgments to tyrannical overseers. Others simply felt stunned and betrayed. Had a lifetime of personal sacrifice and discipline, in all aspects of life, from the most intimate details of sexual relations to the most public aspects of parish religious observances, been rendered meaningless?

Millions of Catholics were in a quandary. Their religion, despite its rigors, had at least proffered the balm of certainty. Now the inconceivable had happened. The fixed and the eternal were neither. In an attempt to check the spread of Vatican II, traditionalists withheld background information about the reforms. By denying laypeople access to the new theology and by preventing them from obtaining the information necessary to come to terms with the profound changes, the traditionalists unwittingly left behind a wake of ruin and confusion from which the Catholic Church and many laypeople have not yet recovered. By telling the story of one man's journey, a journey through the institutional Church as it was in a state of transition, this book provides insight into the post-Vatican II Church, and tells a compelling personal tale along the way.

Joan Schlichte Stockbridge

Introduction

One of the most astonishing events in the history of the Catholic Church was the Second Vatican Council, where an assembly of 2600 bishops voted for radical changes which would turn the ancient structure of the Roman Catholic Church on its head. Among many other reforms, the decrees of Vatican II denied dictatorial authority to popes. From now on, popes and bishops would share authority in order to serve the people. The hitherto imperial church declared itself the servant church. Furthermore, the Council decreed that personal behavior should be governed by the informed conscience of each individual. Blind, unquestioning, unchallenging obedience to dogmatic rules was declared a thing of the past.

These and other radical changes of Vatican II were set in motion by Pope John XXIII in 1962 when he called bishops together from around the world "to let in a little fresh air." Coached by hundreds of assigned expert theologians, the bishops debated issues and then voted for sweeping changes. This Second Vatican Council ranked as the largest and most representative ever held. Accredited non-Catholic observers attended, as did laity and nuns. For the first time in church history, a Council concerned itself with bringing church rules into conformity with the Gospel, rather than settling disputes.

Among the changes, Vatican II declared:

The mission of The Church is to make the history of the human race more human by service to those in need, as well as to preach the Gospel and celebrate the sacraments.

The Church embraces more than the Catholic

Church; it includes Orthodox, Anglicans and Protestants.

Religious truth can be found outside the Church.

No one can be compelled to accept the Christian faith, nor can one be penalized in any way for not being a Christian.

Unfortunately, Pope John XXIII did not live to see the end of the Council. After John XXIII's death, an assembly of Cardinals elected Paul VI as the successor pope. At first Paul VI seemed to support Council reforms; in 1965 he officially endorsed all the decrees promulgated by the Council. However, three years later he licensed bishops to ignore the Council's ban on dictatorial authority. Despite the clear restrictions in papal authority mandated by the Council, Paul VI issued a papal encyclical which unilaterally decreed all forms of artificial birth control to be intrinsically evil. His use of independent authority, despite the decrees of the Council, makes no logical sense until one recognizes him and the bishops as victims of a common organizational pathology whereby rules supplant the purpose of the organization. Rules, initially intended as a means to assist the organization to carry out its purpose, become seen as an end in themselves and eventually smother the originating vision and purpose.

Afflicted with this disease, Pope Paul and other rulekeepers in the church down through the centuries believed that the old rules of authority, which created the organizational structure, were necessary preconditions for preaching the Gospel. In practice, the construct of organizational rules had become a Golden Calf worshipped at the expense of the Church's mission. Caught in this pathology, the rulekeepers had no choice other than to derail Vatican II. This behavior of Pope Paul VI and the bishops introduced dilemma, chaos, and conflict into the way of Roman Catholic life. Worse, the global movement then under way towards a unified Christianity came to a screeching halt.

In the rarefied atmosphere surrounding the Council, bishops had met with the support of designated expert theologians.

The theologians, as a general rule removed from the fray of diocesan politics, enthusiastically and compellingly presented the case for changing old organizational practice. With theological support and encouragement, the bishops scrupulously debated and explored the many gaps between church purpose and church practice. Eventually, they voted to approve the 16 documents of Vatican Council II, which Pope Paul VI then endorsed and promulgated. With official church teaching back on track to conformity with the Gospel, theologians thought fresh air blew through the halls of a musty museum. But they failed to understand the staying power in the musty rules, which is a topic this book will explore.

Organizational rules take on an independent life of their own. Classic organizational theory predicts the fate of substantive rule changes when they hit the warp and woof of operations. The changes die. In the post-Vatican II church, the rule changes were immediately suspect, and "theologian" became a dirty word. Back in their dioceses after the Council, these same bishops who had voted for the 16 decrees found themselves without the support of expert theologians. At first, most of them did nothing to either actively promote the changes or to suppress the changes. Then, they reverted to their former roles as Roman Catholic bureaucrats. They closed ranks in defense of the old rules of authority. When Paul VI issued his encyclical on birth control, *Humanae Vitae,* making it a litmus test of orthodoxy, most of the American Catholic hierarchy lined up in support of the proclamation, thereby implicitly rejecting what Vatican II had stood for. At the time, I thought they were either motivated by outdated theology, insensitive to the need for changes, or part of a plot to hold together the old empire. I now think a pathological addiction to rules at the expense of original goals drove the authority figures in the Roman Catholic Church.

In the following pages, I recount my experiences with line authority in two large scale organizations, the U.S. Navy and the Roman Catholic Church. As explained in the text, the U.S. Naval Academy found and took the antidote for the pathology while the hierarchical church, unfortunately, still suffers from the disease.

My struggles differed little from those of other dedicated Roman Catholics suddenly called to come to grips with conflicts between loyalty to a lifelong dedication to rules and the challenges of the new freedom from rules presented by Vatican II. In my own case, the impetus of Vatican II and exposure to debates among professional theologians made me confront church rules actually in conflict with the Gospel, such as the inequitable treatment of women and the harsh rules for marriage and divorce. When I saw the unilateral action of Paul VI in the matter of birth control, I joined the worldwide chorus of protest. People asked the same question about me as they had asked about the bishops during the Council: "What had gotten into his head?"

I broke free of the organizational rules of the church which had held me firm, like doubled-up docking lines from a ship to the wharf. As a docking line both anchors and tethers a ship, my belief in the rules both constrained and comforted me. At first I believed that rules such as "Attend Mass on Sundays" and "Support your pastor" outlined the behavior necessary to please God. Later, this belief was reinforced by the sacredness attributed to bureaucratic rules by all members of any bureaucracy and resulted in the doubling-up of the line, holding me firmly to the ways of the hierarchical church. After Vatican II, tutored by theologians, I steamed safely past the Scylla of cynicism and the Charybdus of fear to the freedom of the Gospel. In the course of this passage, I mentally separated the hierarchical church from what I thought of as the true Church. I began to think of the hierarchical church of rulekeepers as "The Purple Kingdom"; in contrast, I began to think of The Church as the followers of the Gospel or the People of God.

Some Roman Catholic clergy escaped servitude to the rules. They kept their own counsel. Their approach, like that of Pope John XXIII, tended to be pastoral, rather than organizational. Their direct concerns centered on needs of the human situation, here and now. They tried to make sense out of life rather than defend rules. For example, Cardinal Garrone in Rome, charged with worldwide seminary surveillance, accepted without question my definition of a Roman Catholic as one who considered what the Pope said before making a personal decision in a matter of faith or morals. His endorsement said the

Pope did not have the last word, each individual did. As will be seen in the narrative, the Purple Kingdom could not accept such a definition and demanded my resignation from the Pope John Seminary.

Yet, clearly, the hierarchical Roman Catholic Church does provide meaning and direction in the lives of very many. On the other hand, rules in conflict with both the Gospel and contemporary needs fail to make sense out of life for very many others. My journey may help them to better understand that their situation derives from a perennial dilemma. How can a construct of rules encourage good deeds in the context of free choice?

One of the basic reference points for decision-making is the principle of loving thy neighbor as thyself. One of the functions of organized religion is to help make sense out of life. Perhaps from these common denominators for action a new model can be found for a worldwide Church: a Church that operates on the premise that responsible human behavior can be produced by the rule of informed conscience. Could this be the Vatican II model?

Three Popes in Order of Their Appearance

Pius XII was an intellectual aristocrat who was Pope during WWII. He ate all meals alone. He required authors to deliver wheelbarrows full of reference books with all documents sent for his approval. He telephoned to complain whenever he could not find references quoted in footnotes. He broke the precedent of the voluntary confinement of popes to Vatican City by a trip around the corner to inaugurate a new building of the North American College.

John XXIII succeeded Pius XII. First perceived as a kindly, elderly and interim pope, he displayed good humor and a habit of refreshing wisecracks. The very afternoon of his election, he invited cronies to come in for supper. He took a pastoral rather than a legalistic approach to the papacy. He delegated research to the experts. He summoned all bishops to Rome for Vatican Council II, "to let in a little fresh air." It lasted beyond his lifetime. His informal talks to newly-ordained priests told tales of how he helped people.

After a varied ecclesiastical career, Paul VI succeeded John XXIII as Pope. During the pontificate of Pius XII, the future Paul VI had co-chaired the Secretary of State's Office with Monsignor Tardini. Pius XII summarily removed him from this office under suspect circumstances and demoted him, naming him Archbishop of Milano. John XXIII promoted him to cardinal and referred to him as Hamlet. Paul VI presided over the closing ceremonies of Vatican Council II and promulgated its decrees. His talks to newly-ordained priests emphasized obedience to authority.

State of the Question

Abou Ben Adhem (may his tribe increase!)
Awoke one night from a deep dream of peace.
And saw, within the moonlight in his room,
Making it rich, and like a lily in bloom,
An Angel writing in a book of gold.

Exceeding peace had made Ben Adhem bold.
And to the presence in the room he said,
"What writest thou?" The vision raised its head.
And with a look made of all sweet accord
Answered, "The names of those who love the Lord."

"And is mine one?" said Abou. "Nay, not so,"
Replied the Angel. Abou spoke more low,
But cheerily still, and said "I pray thee then,
Write me as one that loves his fellow men."

The Angel wrote and vanished. The next night
It came again with a great awakening light,
And showed the names whom love of God had
    blessed.
And lo! Ben Adhem's name led all the rest.

—Leigh Hunt

—2—

The Magic of the Rules

Growing up in the 30s, we conformed to the directives of any authority, civil or ecclesiastic. Street car conductors made change, wore caps squarely, had uniforms with shiny buttons and ruled behavior like drill sergeants in a marine boot camp. The desperate financial condition of the times explained some of this conformity. Streetcar conductors' clout came in good part from their status as wage earners.

Employers dictated behavior, sometimes off the job as well. They rationed the great shortage: money. Work for one dollar a day attracted many takers. Bricklayers, hired each day in groups of three, knew the one who set the least number of bricks got the pink slip. Those in the service sector, like my father, a dentist, worked at other tasks. People needed dentists, but few had cash to offer. Returning to the job that had put him through dental school, he went back to the post office to sort mail at night. Years of tight cash always in the control of employers made it clear that the boss is always right. Everybody went by the rules. In public parks and on college campuses, nobody walked across the grass. Everybody stuck to designated paths.

The state of the economy and the power of the rules handed the clergy a stacked deck. Through their prayers, clergy held out hope for a job without having to deliver the contract. If the job came through, their prayers worked. If no job came, God had other plans. Clergy could not lose.

When my father applied for a staff position at one of the hospitals, our family made a novena to one of the Jesuit saints,

2

driving to Holy Trinity every evening for nine consecutive days. We expected effective intercession with God by the saint on my father's behalf. A very formal affair, the novena ritual took place in the always-crowded big upstairs church with music from the grand pipe organ, a sermon by one of the Jesuits in the massive, high pulpit and recitation of special prayers. The big moment came each night when the entire kneeling congregation interrupted the vocal prayer. They bowed heads in silence to make mental mention of their individual petitions. When my father did not get the job, we continued firm in our belief. We knew that God must have better plans for us.

Years later, the popular idea that the Almighty altered the course of history on request got a major overhaul at the Gregorian University in Rome. There, I learned the theology about the utility of such prayers. The purpose of praying was not to make a bargain with God. On the contrary, by praying, a petitioner became disposed to do the things necessary to achieve the desired objective. Cardinal Cushing once expressed similar sentiments to a reporter who asked him whether the Sign of the Cross which a young boxer made would do him any good. "If he can fight, it will," replied the Cardinal. This insight would have come as quite a surprise to my father and family. We depended in a magical way on the efficacy of prayer itself.

Although hard times characterized the 30s, institutional religion thrived. Most people followed religious rules as naturally as they breathed air. Church rules resolved issues with ease and gave certitude as to the will of God. Better than navigators' "Rules of the Road," church rules guaranteed safe passage through the rocks and shoals of life to the great prize of everlasting happiness.

My parents were guided by the Roman Catholic rules of upbringing. Neighborhood schools lacked the resources to meet my parents' standards for behavior and morals. School day mornings, books and lunches in hand, we piled into my father's car. He braved Boston's snarled traffic and delivered us to Holy Trinity Grammar School on the other side of the city. Holy Trinity Parish offered Jesuit learning and discipline. The Sisters of St. Francis ran the grammar school. Besides reading, writing, and arithmetic, the nuns drilled us daily in questions and answers of the *Baltimore Catechism*, so called because the text received the endorsement of Roman Catholic bishops assembled in Baltimore. This catechism contained the approved catalogue of rules on matters religious.

All Roman Catholic education included memorization of the questions and answers of the *Baltimore Catechism*. Public school children were sent to Sunday School where volunteers would drill them, too, in the rules. The volume grew larger as we advanced in grade. Like the multiplication tables, the catechism listed items I had to memorize. As a kid, I simply went along. The Jesuits came in during our drill to add instruction. Visiting missionaries added spice with tales of their adventures in strange lands.

As an adult, I heard bemused criticisms of people in China because they were drilled in the sayings of Chairman Mao. Their rote learning differed little from my own drill in catechism questions and answers. Continuing repetition of identical phrasing riveted the rules in our developing minds. There, they directed our thought processes and shaped our prejudices.

In the days before the recent Vatican Council, Roman Catholics seeking wider intellectual horizons ran into the *Index of Forbidden Books,* which listed all the published material we could not read under pain of mortal sin. Our religious leaders knew right from wrong, truth from untruth, so we were taught, and so we believed. Read any of the forbidden material and you read untruth. Also, you went forever to the fires of hell. One could become truly repentant, go to confession and be forgiven. However, a debt of atonement remained, as it did for all forgiven sins.

Good deeds worked off the debt. A place called purgatory cleared up unpaid balances. There, one stayed in fire until suffering paid off all debt. Vatican Council II wiped out the idea of purgatory. Indulgences died with it. So did prayers for the deceased. Their former meaning and purpose evaporated, new funeral rites directed attention to needs of the living.

Before Vatican II, any published work on faith or morals had to display two endorsements. One came from the bishop's censor of books. The other came from the bishop. The absence of either meant the work lacked orthodoxy. Censorship and fear of hell kept me from testing for truth outside the compound. Besides, I thought life inside the compound made sense.

My generation grew up in a religious ghetto. As work began on Vatican Council II, the *Index of Forbidden Books* disappeared.

Living in the compound, it seemed tragic that members of other religious bodies lacked the benefits of Roman Catholicism. I regretted that some of my best friends did not understand. We never talked about religious differences. We went our serious and separate ways when it came to churchgoing. When I was growing up, clergy and church members wanted no contamination from the rules of other religious bodies. We could not play on ball teams sponsored by non-Catholic churches. I could not join a local Boy Scout troop because of its sponsorship by the Congregational Church. The troop however did provide me with the Scout handbook.

Hidden consequences lurked in this segregated existence. The failure to discuss our religious opinions with others and develop growth from the give-and-take produced stunted personalities. I first noticed them in Rome. When I served on the faculty of the North American College, I spent considerable time with Roman Catholic visitors from the USA, many of them highly-placed in their secular pursuits. I used to marvel at the contrast between their opinionated, grammar-school knowledge of religion and the very sophisticated understanding they showed in areas of secular competence. They mirrored my situation for many years in the Navy, as well as did the rule-bound lives of countless faithful down through the centuries.

Catechism drill, concern for orthodoxy, segregation from other points of view, and the dire consequences for heresy bonded me to the magic rules. Life became a contest between me and forces blocking the road to heaven. Eternal bliss could be mine, if I stuck by the rules. At school, story after story told how the saints stuck by the rules.

For people like my parents, these rules revealed the mind of God. As kids we absorbed their attitudes. Church disciplinary laws, like attend Mass on Sunday, abstain from meat on Friday, and support your pastor, had the equivalent authority of divine laws such as the 10 Commandments. Church rules about marriage and divorce chained many couples to marital warfare. Organizational rules contaminated the simple, straightforward message of the Gospel to love one another.

—3—

The Solace and Meaning in Rules

Dedication to church rules dictated my choice of college. Rule-based religion could never withstand challenges likely to come from uncensored versions of history. Nor could it cope with contrary arguments from philosophers. While convinced of my own lack of knowledge at the time, I thought properly prepared scholars could answer any argument proposed against Roman Catholic doctrine and practice.

Religion and finance combined to direct my choice to Boston College, run by the Jesuits. I could live at home, save the expense of board and room and get a good solid grounding in Roman Catholic teachings, along with my course in higher education. I chose pre-med, applied and Boston College accepted me. However, just before graduation from high school, a longshot alternative came through. I won an appointment to the United States Naval Academy. Torn between two service career paths, I opted for the Navy. Finances really tipped the scale. The federal government took care of all the bills. At the height of the Great Depression, with three sisters and two brothers in the pipeline for college, one free tuition put less strain on scarce family financial resources.

In June 1939, a block of about 20 young men completed the processing and assembled in civilian clothes on the marble steps inside the big rotunda of Bancroft Hall, the dormitory building. We took an oath to defend the Constitution of the

United States. An extremely brief but sharply-focused welcoming speech set the ground rules.

"Take a look at the man on your right. Now take a look at the man on your left. One of you will not graduate. March off."

We traded civilian clothes for military uniforms, got shots and short haircuts, joined with others already processed, and found ourselves in a big, brand-new world.

The welcoming prediction proved accurate. One-third of us gave up before graduation. We learned to march, drill, navigate, sail, and shoot. We enjoyed dry bunks, hot showers, and meals served with linen napkins. Nobody asked about our wants and needs; others set the standards and the pace. We measured up.

Life under military discipline differed little from full-time compliance with the Roman Catholic religion. Rules engulfed us. Both institutions survived and functioned through unquestioning obedience to line authority. Both required obeisance to authority figures, and a large dose of fear of higher-ups permeated the ranks in both. The Academy and the Church made a virtue of obedience. The Church held out rewards and punishment for a future life. The Navy dished them out on the spot.

An impersonal and mechanical quality characterized our academic study. The total number of pages in textbooks, divided by the number of class days in a semester, yielded daily assignments. Faculty served mainly as referees between students and grade books. Daily quizzes got scored in every course. They counted two-thirds of total semester grades, which got rank-ordered, published on bulletin boards and mailed to our parents or guardians. Academic freedom to choose came only once: we were allowed to pick a foreign language. Self-reliance became a key resource in an atmosphere of continuing competition. Math classes gave the vivid example. At blackboards around the room, we worked out problems in the assigned text. The instructor simply walked around and checked off correct answers. To suddenly find myself struggling in a long-term, impersonal program of relentless competition made life grim. A new challenge sat on the table, one I would meet over and over again: demonstrate my worth to a new audience. Evaluated constantly, graded by all our seniors on our aptitude for the service, the pressure never let up.

The Academy introduced me to life in a total institution. Besides board and room, it prescribed personal behavior and lifestyle. It took considerable self-discipline to go along with the rules, even though I was conditioned to comply with any authority, parental, civil, or church. The bad economic conditions bolstered my moments of sagging motivation. College education here came free-of-charge, with a paying job at the end of the line.

Years later, I again encountered the authority of a total institution when I attended a seminary. This time, although equally dictatorial and with rules even more intrusive into personal behavior and lifestyle, I did not experience the same sense of aloneness. For one thing, competition remained covert. Besides, individually, we made direct contact with the very top of the pyramid, God Himself. The sense of collaboration with the Almighty for the benefit of the human race gave crystal-clear meaning, direction, and value to the effort. A similar sentiment of dedication to a cause bigger than myself made service in the Navy more attractive when the United States declared war on Japan.

In retrospect, both institutions proved sanguine about individuals and interested in survival of the organization. The Navy demonstrated more consideration for its operatives, however, while the church left the matter in the hands of God. We used to say the Navy figured out how to put gun platforms at sea and then considered where to put the humans. But the Navy offered rehabilitation programs, pension benefits, and medical care. Due process existed, side-by-side with dictatorial authority. The Church either got the performance it was looking for or you ended up on the sidewalk, looking for help. Due process in the Church amounted to pleading your case before the bishop as sole judge and jury.

Nobody at the Academy cared what religion you espoused. The *Index of Forbidden Books* meant as little here as a foxhole on the deck of a warship. The technically-oriented curriculum left no space for philosophical speculation. Midshipmen simply declared for one organized religion and attended its services. I attended St. Mary's, the local Catholic church. It provided a touch of hometown comfort. The welcome familiarity of ritual and rules gave balm to my psyche, frayed by loneliness in a competitive world. The Catholic midshipmen mustered and marched there each Sunday morning. Since the church could not hold all of us at once, one morning a month our battalion went to late Mass. It was there I discovered the first chink in what I had hitherto considered a perfect system.

The black parishioners sat by themselves, segregated in the back of the church. Such a discriminatory practice clashed with my belief in the universal sameness of church rules. I also believed in the equality of all humans before the Almighty. I complained to the priest assigned by the parish for midshipmen affairs. He did not like it either, but accepted it as part of the status quo those days in the South. Today, I see the practice as an example of goal displacement by the rules.

Why did the Church tolerate slavery in the first place? It defies reason to make a case for any human's need to be enslaved by another. More likely, the leadership in the early Christian Church suffered from the disease inherent in the very process of getting organized. In order to organize, rules were needed to give structure to the early church. They spelled out job descriptions. They said who reported to whom. With the rules came their inherent dynamic to become the purpose, which meant that survival of the institution eventually took precedence over its purpose.

In the early Church, if the clergy had preached against the exploitation of slaves, arguing that the Gospel dictated loving thy neighbor as thyself, the masters would have rebelled. The Church needed the resources of the masters to sustain the organization. What to do? Church leaders, already afflicted with the rule-born disease, necessarily thought it impossible to preach the Gospel without the structure created by the rules. Forced to judge their house of rules indispensable, they saw little choice. Love of neighbor lost to a new rule: slaves, obey your masters. The masters kept their slaves, the slaves got rewarded in the next life, the organization survived. Only the mission of the Church lost out.

Love of neighbor got sold out to enhance the organization. The rules overtook the purpose of the Church. Anyone who thinks a Divine Hand guided these official decisions has a dilemma. Either God Almighty wanted slavery or Roman Catholic organizational behavior through the centuries suffered from the same affliction as secular organizations. To deliberately promote exploitation of one human by another, as we read in St. Paul's dictum for slaves to obey their masters, contradicts the Gospel message. This leaves the pathology of goal displacement by the rules as the explanation for the Catholic Church's toleration of slavery. Church leaders suffered the same affliction as their secular counterparts.

Vatican II provided the antidote to purge this pathology of takeover by the rules. It proclaimed a new set of operating principles in tune with both the Church's mission and the world's environment. It declared the Church to be the Servant of the People. In theory, at least, the black parishioners could not be told to sit in the back of the church. They could tell the bishops and clergy where to sit.

As a midshipman at St. Mary's in Annapolis, I knew nothing about the ability of rules to wreck the purpose of an organization. I only knew something was fouled up, and I did not like it. At the late Mass, a few midshipmen always sat in the back pews. Nobody said a word. World War II soon became my real world and drove these concerns from my mind.

The bombing of Pearl Harbor ratcheted life and routine into newly-energized channels. With a war to win, my prior sense of isolation ceded to a sense of collective and united purpose. The Navy became my life's all-embracing priority. Competition continued, tempered now by a sense of national togetherness for a good cause.

World War II made military duty seem noble, imperative, a response to a clear national need bigger than myself. Serving during the war, I felt proud to be part of a great cause. Years hence, the Roman Catholic Church assumed a similar domination in my life. After World War II, the Church attracted many veterans who wanted to continue finding fulfillment through service to others. The extraordinary number of veterans enrolled in seminaries after the war supports this thesis.

Assigned to the *USS Philadelphia,* a light cruiser on duty in the Atlantic, I reported on board in June 1942, a green ensign, 21 years of age, eager to do my part in the vast war effort of the country. As the next 39 months unfolded, I lucked out. I met and worked with an extraordinary array of talented people who helped me at every turn. I enjoyed bonds of friendship founded on mutual support and interdependence in times of great physical danger. Senior officers, uniformly firm but friendly, exercised leadership through service and technical know-how.

The ship went through the Atlantic and Mediterranean theaters of war unscathed, earned five campaign ribbons, fought off 36 direct air assaults and received a Navy Unit Citation for exemplary service. We gained some notoriety in the *Stars and Stripes*, the army newspaper, as the Galloping Ghost of the Sicilian Coast, thanks to numerous reports on German radio of our sinking.

A first pleasant surprise came when I learned the ship carried a Catholic chaplain, a Jesuit from New York by the name of Dan Burke. I attended Mass every day, something impossible to do before. It took only a walk to a midship office space, just below the main deck. The presence of a Catholic chaplain assured me of proper linkage to the Almighty. Not only could I pick up all these easy credits for daily Mass, but also a general absolution from all my sins whenever we entered a dangerous combat situation. According to my rule-managed and simplistic belief, my private world stood in good shape. My energies impacted directly on actions to make the world right again, and the chaplain's presence assured my safe entry into the next world, in the event such a transition happened. The Linus blanket of religious rules glossed over the grim reality of our wartime cruising. I merrily went about the business of acquiring the skills for professional naval positions, such as radio officer, assistant navigator, officer of the deck, division officer, and gunnery control officer.

Religious beliefs rarely became subjects of conversation. I never sensed religious affiliation affected any decision of a senior officer. Besides, a recognized code said never to discuss politics or religion in the ward room where the 106 officers socialized and ate. We sat on aluminum armchairs at four long, linen-covered tables, in strict seniority by date of commission. Mess attendants set our personal napkin rings at our places in the proper pecking order. The time just before and after meals occasioned discussion across and within departmental lines. Decision-makers listened and exchanged ideas with junior officers. While ideas flowed freely, strict codes of behavior prevailed. No one sat down until the executive officer did, or sent word to do so. Neither did anyone leave the table until the exec signaled the end of the meal. We always wore the uniform of the day.

These friendly and informal exchanges with superiors about operational matters set up a lifetime habit. I always felt at ease in the presence of seniors. Rather than think about the rank of the decision-maker, I thought about the problem at hand and saw myself as part of the decision-making process. My experiences on the *Philadelphia* also taught me to first attribute foul-ups to human error, rather than to immediately assume some Machiavellian maneuvers. To correct foul-ups, I first got the attention of the offenders. Once lined up, sailors could be given the lecture necessary to dispel ignorance or overcome lethargy. Petty officers, who knew the ropes, could be very persuasive to their charges. They helped many avoid more serious motivators, like extra duty, fines, or even the brig.

Vatican Council II lacked the petty officers to encourage bishops to act according to its decrees. Bishops got the lecture during the Council. However, most then went back home to business as usual and convinced themselves they had learned all they needed when they had been students sitting in seminary classrooms. When theologians, who knew the ropes, published new texts based upon the documents of the Council, the theological void in the bishops' backgrounds caused them to panic, close ranks and stick by the old rules, the only ones they understood. Had there been some method to dispel their ignorance, lethargy, or fear, the course of outcomes from Vatican II would have cleaned out the outdated rules accumulated over the centuries. A new set of rules would have put the worldwide operation of the Church on its proper track toward the Gospel's objective. New rules, adapted to the current human condition, would have directed Catholic energies to the needs of neighbors now.

Instead, sad to say, bishops stuck their heads under the tent of tradition. Mesmerized by the old rules, they strayed further and further from the Gospel mission. Curiously, while trapped by the rules, they thought they traveled on the side of the angels. Therein sat a central malaise.

Certain activities aboard ship demanded absolute conformity to established rules. I launched aircraft as a catapult control officer. I also recovered aircraft as officer of the deck. Never once did I deviate from any item on the check-off list. I also organized hours and hours of repetitious drill on a gun-loading training machine. The 15-man, five-inch gun crews drilled so often and repeated so precisely the same moves that muscle memory carried them through the confusion and smoke of battle. Each man functioned as a repetitive unit in an efficient machine. Only control officers made decisions. The gun crews did two things. They went into action and they ceased fire.

I think conservative bishops viewed themselves as control officers in life's battles against the powers of darkness. They presumed us so well-drilled in Catholic obedience that we needed only two choices, act according to their check-off list of rules, or not to act at all. At sea, safety required following precisely the check-off list for launching and recovery of aircraft. To coordinate sailors' actions while big guns thundered over their heads required simplicity of choice: act or not act. Those same sailors could not use such pre-programmed behavior in their personal lives. The drills and check-off lists functioned as a straightjacket, limiting options. Today, people face complex variables to weigh and evaluate before deciding on personal action steps. Now, only they have the data to function as control officers of their lives.

The *Philadelphia* furnished fire support during 10 days and nights for the invasion of Italy at Salerno. We could see German tanks explode on the beach after hits by our guns. A radio-controlled bomb missed us, exploded close aboard, lifted our stern high out of the water, and warped a propeller shaft. During the same incident, a pilot made a diving run on us. We threw everything we could at him and missed. Luckily, so did he. As he leveled out and streaked broadside along the water, he slid his canopy back and gave us a big wave. We all waved back. No hard feelings, just doing our respective jobs. Like professional fighters in a draw match, we saluted each other.

That salute changed my perception of the war. Suddenly, I saw us as gladiators in an arena, with others placing bets on us, a grim and crazy situation. Previously, in my battle station on the sky director, with no personal desire to engage in deadly combat with anyone, I had dueled with every unfriendly warplane in my sector of the sky. Until the moment when the pilot saluted us, my thoughts concentrated merely on my development of skills as a professionally-competent naval officer. Suddenly, I saw myself as a pawn in the chess game others played, with the German pilot and myself at the mercy of decisions made by others. We could do precious little about it. The immediate need to defend the ship against other pilots pushed these fleeting thoughts into my subconscious, where they stayed. A civilian observer occasioned their reawakening. Toward the end of the war, he asked what my plans were. I never thought of such a question. The image of myself as a pawn then moved to the front burner.

Close to the end of the war, an overnight liberty from Naples to Rome found me standing in St. Peter's basilica, just before Pope Pius XII entered. The vast and lengthy nave lacked benches and pews. Instead, four-foot-high wooden barriers formed a wide corridor, crowded on both sides, six to ten deep, with a mix of civilians, nuns, clerics, and thousands of GIs. Standing in the rear, I faced the corridor as the Pope entered the long nave. Wearing a white cassock, white sash, and white skull cap, he sat on a red upholstered throne mounted on a platform which was carried on the shoulders of six men in scarlet uniforms. He moved energetically from side to side, leaning over the arms of his chair to touch the outstretched sea of arms and hands, while the six men in scarlet continued their steady advance. He smiled so affably that at first I thought he'd spotted long-lost friends in the back of the church. He radiated genuine warmth. Soon I realized I stood in the midst of a cheering crowd. Such behavior ran counter to my training. One kept silent in church. Here, in the headquarters of the entire Roman Catholic world, people acted like they were at a political rally, and the Pope was like a politician out to meet the voters.

Despite my initial irritation with the noisy behavior, I stood in profound awe in the presence of the one man in the whole world whom I thought stood in for God. What the clergy told us came from him. When he spoke, God spoke. Lines of strain highlighted his sharp-featured face. His wire rimmed glasses stood out. He obviously wanted to greet everyone in the basilica. He worked at touching the outstretched hands. I wondered how he and God communicated. His eagerness to reach out to individual hands surprised me. Such behavior ran contrary to what I had expected, given the above-human stature I ascribed to him and the aloofness of other authority figures in the church.

Once the Pope disappeared down the nave, I left to see the town. The U.S. Army had arranged transportation, and the USO had made reservations for our meals and lodging. Spared from the war's destruction, the shrines of ancient Rome, the Vatican Museum, and the catacombs got a hasty inspection. I saw much to report to the homefront. It all paled before the big news. I had seen the Pope, the embodiment of all the power and authority of the Church, including its rules. Little did I imagine the day to come when I was to stand watch at the foot of his death bed, as dignitaries paid their last respects.

Soon after my visit to Rome, the *Philadelphia* entered drydock in Gibraltar to fix the propeller shafts damaged at Salerno. We exchanged visits with the *Uganda*, a British cruiser. A pattern soon developed: drinks on the *Uganda*, dinner and movies on the *Philadelphia*. In three weeks we wiped out their entire year's liquor quota. The U.S. Navy ran on dry. The Royal Navy carried spirits. On the *Philadelphia*, Captain Ansel brought us the closest to wet. While he respected Navy rules, he managed not to let them interfere with the welfare of the crew. The beer available in Mediterranean ports was awful, by our standards. On one of our visits to the States, he ordered beer stored under the hangar deck and the hatch locked. An armed marine on duty prevented access. In Mediterranean ports, a flat barge tied up alongside. After we off-loaded, watch sections took turns going over the side for a beer run, thereby complying with the Navy prohibition against consuming alcohol aboard ship. The need to climb back up wobbly cargo nets kept sobriety at the appropriate level.

In the bay of Gibraltar, I took part in a three-crew sailing contest between the *Uganda*, the *Philadelphia*, and the Wrens from the shore station. The Wrens, the British equivalent of the Waves, the women in the U.S. Navy, won. We threw a dance for them in the ward room. One of them was so tall I had to signal her to duck whenever we approached a ventilator shaft.

We left Gibraltar, got repaired in Philadelphia, and lent support to the invasion at Southern France. Allied victory came clearly into sight. The hitherto high intensity of life at sea slowed. The Navy and the world headed for an entirely new ballgame. Signals of impending change came clearly as we criss-crossed the Atlantic on various missions, like escorting President Truman to the Potsdam Conference. The *Philadelphia* waited for the President's return to Antwerp in Belgium. There, we inspected a recently-liberated concentration camp. Rooms and corridors smelled of fresh whitewash, obliterating wartime messages and graffiti. As I stood in the chamber where some Belgians had kept favor with the Nazis by torturing other Belgians, I was deeply moved. The experience ranked with the profound moment when I'd seen the Pope in person. In the Pope, I saw the embodiment of good. In this chamber, I saw the embodiment of evil, a world gone insane.

To clear the world of such evil had been the mission of our military might. In contrast to my *Philadelphia* shipmates, a number of the war-torn Belgians lost their sense of interdependence. They became mutually destructive, split apart into fighting factions. Some collaborated with the invading German army; others resisted. The concentration camp operated under the direction of a single German official. He, we heard, took no part in the actual torture of Belgians. Collaborating Belgians did the dirty work. The invading Allied army smashed this Belgian cycle of self-annihilation.

On a couple of subsequent trips across the Atlantic, I stood watch in the sky director, high above the water, with an unobstructed view of the sky. Nobody expected an air attack. Our plot of German submarine locations also showed less and less activity. Gunnery watch duty functioned more as a precaution than as active defense against an expected attack. Morpheus presented the greater threat. Generally, we followed the Gulf Stream with its blue waters and balmy weather. At night, the phosphorescent wake trailed off to the horizon and sparkled beneath millions of stars. Larger than life questions surfaced naturally. I found myself wondering how the war related to all that silent splendor. What would the world be like after the war? Should I stay in the Navy? If I got out, what would I do? Did God have any direction for me? I believed the Almighty intervened in human affairs to the extent of having laid out a plan for each person. Where did I fit? I never gave this question any thought before, but now during the quiet night watches, round and round these questions went. My religious training helped little with this quandary, other than to affirm that human destiny somehow related to all that splendor in the sky.

Reflections on Antwerp's concentration camp occupied much of my now-plentiful quiet time at sea. I could understand how individuals attacked one another. I could understand how one army attacked another. But here, people of the same nation and city tortured their own. Worse, they did so for the benefit of an invading enemy, bent on imposing servitude. I heard of similar behavior in other invaded European countries. How could humans be so inhuman? The torture stopped with the vanquished Nazis, but the same people remained in every country. Could the fragile fabric of human relations be mended? Would the new world coming together really make matters any different? I hoped so. After all, we considered World War II as the war to end all wars.

Convinced that mankind could develop a world of mutual support, I wanted to be part of the team to create such a community. One point became clear. I could not stay in the Navy; the only reason for continuing would be job security. I thought that not reason enough. I continued unresolved about what I would do. Although closely allied to the Roman Catholic Church, I had never considered the seminary as a possible option. The mother of an assistant pastor in my hometown brought the subject to my attention. Her son frequented our house when I went to high school. He often took me to Boston Red Sox games. On one leave from the ship, I visited his mother to pay my respects. She told me he thought I should have gone to the seminary instead of the Naval Academy. At the time, I took her remarks as a nice compliment but thought the moment for such a move had long passed. Her words surfaced when I began to think about my part in the new forum in which mankind could achieve the hope and ambition for a better world.

My thoughts about the future drifted from practical considerations about employment to philosophical questions. What could put the pieces together after the war? Contrasting mental pictures of the Pope embodying good and the concentration camp symbolizing evil stayed in my head. To tackle the grand issues of life as a full-time occupation became an attractive option. Besides, I did not want to be anybody's pawn in a chess game over which I lacked control. To work directly for good in place of evil soon became my life's ambition. My employer would be no less than God. I gave no thought to authority figures like cardinals, bishops and pastors.

The projected massive enrollments in colleges by veterans no longer made study at a seminary an impractical idea. Completely mesmerized by my own version of religious reality, I saw the Catholic Church and its system of rules as eminently suited to rebuild the world into a community of mutual support. Never once did I question how the Roman Catholic religion functioned in war-torn Belgium, or in Nazi circles. I believed in the Church's divine mission to promote a worldwide community of people who loved one another. As I write, I wonder what paralyzed the Roman Catholic hierarchy in Germany before, during and after discovery of the concentration camps. Why did it require the force of the civil arm to eradicate such blatant violation of the Church's primary mission? I venture the hypothesis that goal displacement by the rules tied the hands of the German hierarchy.

Roman Catholic leaders in Germany, blinded by behavior riveted to rules of the organization, failed to face the enormity of the evil under their very noses. Organizational survival forced the sell-out of the Gospel to the rules, not unlike the sell-out to slavery by the early Church. Had the German hierarchy acted to promote the Gospel, even at the expense of considerable organizational turmoil, history might well have missed at least the gross horrors of the camps.

I saw Roman Catholic rules as the way to organize humans in their best interests. The lengthy seminary course in philosophy, theology, and scripture was clearly intended to teach future priests how to make sense out of life. There remained the issue of celibacy, a fixed cost of doing business the Roman Catholic way. I saw no value in it. It did not fit with my earlier image of myself as a married civilian. Eventually I capitulated; otherwise I could not access Roman Catholic resources. The mechanics followed. Immediately after the surrender of Japan, the Secretary of the Navy released me in time to catch the opening of the 1945 academic year at St. John's Seminary in Boston, Mass.

—4—

Rules Structure Behavior

The traditional metamorphosis of caterpillar into butterfly got reversed in my transformation from naval officer to seminarian. Off came the gold braid and the colorful ribbons with stars representing combat services. Black buttons replaced the gold. Instead of a navy uniform, I wore a plain black suit for street wear. For the next six years of seminary training, church rules would bind me like a wrapped-up mummy. The secular world suddenly vanished. Notified of an award of the Bronze Star Medal with combat "V," I wrote to have it mailed to my home address. Now, only the structured church mattered. My new daily uniform signaled my separation from the secular world. My cassock, a long black robe, descended to the ankles. A built-in collar hooked it at the top and a sash tied it at the middle. As a recruit in ecclesiastical boot camp, walled in the compound and outfitted in strange clothes, I felt embarrassed at my situation. I hoped people understood. Some of my former shipmates did not. They tried to contact me and got as far as a member of the faculty, who told them to write me a letter; no visitors were allowed.

Nevertheless, I thought my course properly set for the long haul. Once these training inconveniences became history, my energies would replace evil with good. I could help a lot of people make sense out of life. More importantly, I could help them save their souls. Temporarily, as a seminary student, all my authority vanished. Others held responsibility for operations. I no longer took part in the decision-making. These valued and large chunks of my life became abandoned property. Plebe status started again. With no credibility in this new organization, I began once again to demonstrate my worth. It felt like my stay at the Naval Hospital in Philadelphia. Admitted for treatment of pneumonia, I gave up my uniform and authority as a line officer. Dressed in hospital johnny and bathrobe, I became subject to physicians' directives. The prospect now of six whole years under such control did not fill me with joy. However, convinced that I lacked necessary knowledge and that my new managers knew what I needed, I determined to hang in there.

The isolation did remove distractions. Convinced God watched too, my energies went into high gear. The vast majority of the seminarians impressed me as bright. Their friendliness stood out. As the years went past, I developed great respect for their many talents. As I look back now, I clearly see that later career paths within the Church stunted their growth. The dearth of outlets imposed by organizational rules trapped most of them into marking time in place.

Several other veterans joined the seminary at the same time. With food good and plentiful, quarters warm, dry and quiet, sleep all night every night and neither watches to stand nor miserable work details to duck, we thought seminary lifestyle quite good. The aloofness of faculty contrasted with the accessibility to authority I'd grown used to on board ship, symptomatic of lack of faculty training in uses of authority. Aloofness provided a safe haven. Years of exposure to such role models helped me understand the aloofness demonstrated by many clergy and most bishops. Thankfully, none of the faculty acted like drill sergeants. Mail provided our only contact with the world around us. Cut off from newspapers, secular magazines, radio and telephone, I became so immersed in academic pursuits I failed to reflect on the merits of either isolation from the secular world, or the validity of the training system itself. Besides, I came with a bias in favor of authority.

Seminary routine on class days paralleled that of the Naval Academy. On weekends, the styles sprang apart. The Navy suspended routine from Saturday noon until supper time Sunday. Interactions with the outside world took place, from movies to athletic events to visits and formal dances. We even took visitors sailing on Chesapeake Bay. The seminary rules offered no such relief. Saturdays were class days. On Sundays we attended liturgical ceremonies. Thursdays, days off from classes, we marched off campus in black suits with Roman collars and were assigned to groups for walks through the streets. We hiked under strict orders not to enter stores, offices, or residences. At the time, I couldn't figure out why we got herded along sidewalks for a weekly airing, but later I understood that physical isolation was supposed to lessen contamination by worldly influences. Many years later, I proposed to Cardinal Cushing that he sell the seminary property to Boston College. Were the Boston seminarians to enroll there for studies, I thought the cocoon might be breached by some realism. He thought the conservatives would run him out of town. Today I translate that reaction as a result of fear of female contacts, women being the greatest threat to a celibate clergy.

The extent to which the Catholic bureaucracy feared women became clearer when I went to Italy, whence came seminary regulations. In Italy, seminarians began their studies in the fifth grade. Italian clergy, trained from childhood in female avoidance, made the vast majority of Church rules. Self-justification forced them to esteem celibacy as a superior virtue. They imposed rules to promote it. The rules dictated adversarial roles, even in the scheme of salvation. St. Paul gave them a good start when he declared women should be in church with their heads covered and their mouths shut. How such rules help women make sense out of life bewilders me. The status of women came from an outrageous assumption. Only the male of the species is genetically endowed to make correct decisions. No doubt, celibacy also supported the physical plant. It eliminated inheritance problems, provided cheap help, and allowed the purple kingdom to accumulate peacefully its property assets. It also made busy work. It offered oceans of space to extol the virtues of celibacy and exhort its observance. These more mature reflections did not enter my mind during my years in the seminary. Then I looked at celibacy as the cost of enlistment.

In the seminary, the two-year philosophy course opened new worlds of thought. Our long history of struggle to understand human nature fascinated me. The slow rate of improved understanding surprised me. The far more rapid pace of the hard sciences puzzled me. Logically, humans should have figured themselves out first. It struck me as odd that Thomas Aquinas still dominated the scene so completely. I wondered why so few intellectual giants had emerged through the years. Today I wonder whether Church attitudes which considered human life as a transitionary state to the next world killed off investigation into human nature down through the centuries. Given a deposit of faith, which proclaimed the Good News of salvation, believers assumed nothing else mattered. Life on earth lasted fleetingly. The real concern concentrated on getting to life in eternity. So thought my professors and so did I.

An undeclared assumption held that the dynamics of the secular world could be bent to behave according to Church rules. We did not realize that we played the game backwards. We should have studied ways to integrate the deposit of faith with the real world. Therein stood the task for religious leadership. This objective struggled long to rise to my conscious awareness. Brought up to think the Church knew all the answers, I now think the hierarchical church, trapped by its rules, has yet to learn the questions.

After two years of philosophy came the four-year course of theology. Classes consisted of memory exercises rather than analytical challenges. I did not perceive it then, but the curriculum offered little more than an expanded version of the *Baltimore Catechism*. We really got exercised in the rules. Classes and the daily routine became monotonous, like going through infantry drill every day. Issues, like the concentration camp in Belgium, never made it to the classroom. Bored, I tried to remain interested by studying multi-volume Latin tomes of ceremonial rules.

Happily, a dramatic change brewed when I was offered a transfer to the North American College in Rome, Italy. When notice of the possible transfer arrived at the seminary, I quickly accepted the offer. The faculty of the Boston seminary, stuck in the mud of established decision-making rules, could not fathom how I could so quickly make a decision that would affect the rest of my life. One of the faculty asked what my parents thought about the offer. I informed him I had no idea, but would give them the news of my move as soon as I saw them. He appeared shocked, even offended, and asked how I could make such a decision without their consent.

To me, study in Rome appeared eminently desirable. As a war veteran of adult age, reasonably competent and willing, I knew my mind. Yet the seminary faculty expected me to consult with my parents, my pastor, and advisor and obtain approval from all of them before making such a momentous commitment. In retrospect, I realize the faculty expected me to undergo the tortuous decision-making process characteristic of men in a training program designed for grammar school kids. Any matter for thought or action outside the prescribed routine required exhaustive consultation, and all decision-making was seen as risky and potentially dangerous.

Seminary training in Rome gave my studies a new flavor and focus. Drill in the rules continued, but at least the setting opened my eyes. Similarly strict house rules and routine prevailed, but sight-seeing in the city went with the setting. We lived in one downtown building and went to another for classes. In a sense, the city was the campus. We did daily tours, assigned to groups and dressed in the distinctive garb of the North American College. Our navy blue cassocks displayed sky blue edging with three blue buttons at the top. A red sash around the waist dropped to the right knee.

Appearances were heavily emphasized by the faculty. Every cleric on the street had to wear a big-brimmed black hat and cassock. Each national college had its own distinctive colors. Students even wore their cassocks while playing basketball or soccer, except for the Americans, who simply peeled them off, much to the disbelief of uninitiated Italian observers. They equated this disrobing with abandonment of the clerical life. One of the first student conferences I heard dealt with instructions to keep the cassock on in barber shops. Complaints had been registered about the Americans' scandalous practice of hanging the cassock on a hook before climbing into the barber's chair. One Italian asked me whether American priests could marry. Asked why the question was raised, he replied they often wore long pants under the cassock. Italian clerics never did so. Laity associated long trousers with a life apart from the cassock.

Italian disbelief in the American clergy's obligation to celibacy became complete whenever they encountered us on summer vacations. We wore civilian clothes, a seminary rule I thought made the most sense. It allowed travel without a display of religious profession. Clerical garb is appropriate for ceremony and ceremonial displays. On the street, I thought it advertised religion as being outside the flow of real life. Uniforms serve the purpose of clearly identifying functionaries, such as police. Any public interest reason to identify the profession of cleric escaped me. I thought it related to behavior control.

Actually, the Americans followed a double standard, one in Italy and one in the USA. While we could adopt a common-sense approach to the Italian dress code, upon graduation we failed to confront other unreasonable church rules in the United States. Faced with even more outrageous organizational rules in the pastoral ministry, like those about marriage and divorce, or solemn funerals, we complied with church authority. Cultural differences supplied a partial explanation.

Italians saw the cassock as the dress for a way of life; whereas, the American seminarians saw it simply as a liturgical garment. When we went on duty in the States, conformity to all rules became a necessity. Organizational integrity required us to think in terms of 100% compliance, like the need for water-tight doors on a warship. We saw ourselves under siege by the mentality of the secular world, as well as in competition with other religious bodies.

In a similar vein, the majority of American graduate students studied canon law, which detailed the structure of rules and how the system worked. Theology, on the other hand, interested the Europeans. It dealt with how reason reflecting on faith could make sense out of life. This seemed to me a curious reversal as I thought Americans needed study in how to make sense out of life, while Europeans held a greater stake in how to keep the institution in place.

American Catholics, inheritors of democratic ideas and freedom of speech notwithstanding, usually seemed conscious of their minority status in the largely Protestant United States. They perceived themselves as operating in a hostile environment. Unconsciously, they circled the wagons by thorough application of rules. Cardinal Dougherty of Philadelphia, noted for the numbers of clergy he sent to study canon law, explained it as the simplest way to maintain order and discipline. Also, as the aspiring knew, most American bishops came from ranks of the canon lawyers.

On the other hand, European Catholics enjoyed a mature, well-established, publicly-accepted social place. They lacked interest in 100% conformity. The Latin countries especially ignored body counts and demonstrated little concern for competition from other religious bodies. The Europeans saw religion as being fixed at birth. European seminarians, unconcerned about water-tight doors, concentrated on better understanding of theology. In their minds, the organization sat there as a perennial given. The Americans made no such assumption. An American passion for conformity also helps explain these differences. Illustrative is the chancery office. In Rome, it served strictly as a depository of official documents. In the USA, it held also the seat of executive power. It made, interpreted, and enforced rules. In the States, the chancellor advanced from mere archivist to executive vice president of the diocese in charge of the rules. A chancellor watched each diocese, and the Apostolic Delegate, the Pope's liaison officer in Washington, watched chancellors and bishops. We all marched to the cadence of the rules of canon law.

In retrospect, emphasis on the rules proved disastrous for the church in the USA. Primarily dedicated to the rules of canon law, and with little interest in theological speculation, bishops of the United States drifted without anchors in the stream of discussion during Vatican II. Consultant theologians, knowledgeable of theology's underpinning, pointed out new approaches to old values and identified gaps between old rules, the Gospel, and the times in which people lived. The assembled bishops listened, debated, and voted changes which the Pope endorsed. Vatican II, ideally, should have been followed in every diocese by publication of a new catechism, a step which would have changed the rules worldwide. Only the Church in the Netherlands published a revised catechism. The other rule-keepers could not stomach the changes.

The Gregorian University taught theology. Students came from either national colleges or residences of the various religious orders. National colleges housed those destined to serve as parish clergy. Residences of religious orders held those living under vows and governing some type of community lifestyle and church mission. Jesuits, mostly from Europe, taught the classes. They lectured in Latin. For the first few months, classes were nightmarish: a jumble of unintelligible noise. Once the ear learned to distinguish the sounds, the problem became to refrain from translation into English. Then, comprehension settled in. Classes became productive. The few Americans on the faculty of the Gregorian ranked as the easiest to understand. We rated the Italians from Sicily as being the most difficult, closely followed by the Spanish Jesuits.

One of the lecture halls held about 300 students in an amphitheater with a very large lectern. One day a professor lectured on ascetical theology. He came from Belgium. As an aside remark to a particular point, he observed that it was morally wrong to cheat in an examination. Pandemonium broke out in the hall. Students hissed, stamped their feet, and pounded their desks. They booed the professor. The American students sat aghast. The professor waited out the storm, glared students into silence, and appealed to the voice of authority. "As the professor of ascetical theology," he declared, "I am telling you. It is morally wrong to cheat in an examination. Furthermore," he added, "some people, especially the Americans, consider it a grave defect in a person's character."

The students from the Latin countries did not buy it; neither did some of the professor's own countrymen who had to earn high grades or return to Belgium. They considered an examination an unjust aggressor, to be overcome by any means. Notwithstanding the comments from the professor, cheating attitudes prevailed as always. The Gregorian regularly assigned proctors to patrol the aisles during written examinations. Major subjects got examined orally, one-on-one in Latin, across the desk from the professor.

Similar contrasting attitudes related to punishment for tax evasion. Genuine astonishment registered with every news report of a citizen of the United States jailed by the IRS. The European seminarians also generally disapproved of the war crimes trials held right after World War II. They generally felt that such great disruptions had occurred during the war that no possibility existed to reestablish justice. The sensible course was to close out that chapter of history without reprisals and get on with the business of the day. I thought immediately of the whitewashed walls and corridors of the liberated concentration camp in Antwerp.

My greatest jolt came from Pappy Hurth, the foremost moral theologian in the University and confessor to the Pope. He told the class he did not know whether a particular behavior was immoral. The walls of my authoritarian church with all the answers crashed. Indeed, the more I learned, the more I saw of gray in the world. With new understandings, my innocent perceptions of earlier years evolved into a better awareness of the realities and rules of organized religion. The blissful uncomplicated religious faith of my youth vanished forever. But my uncritical commitment to the Roman Catholic Church and its organization as structured by its rules remained as firm as ever.

I believed that somehow the world had to come around until human behavior fit the ideal codified in church rules. But, in fact, rules went beyond the bounds of faith and morals. Bishops and clergy in the United States also convinced the faithful of their obligation to support the church with cash donations. These donations were then used as the local authority decreed. How did such absolute control get established?

The historical explanation starts when people elected the first bishops. Bound by decrees promulgated to promote the Gospel, bishops enforced rules carefully. Rules defined job descriptions, which included scope of authority. Over time, as circumstances changed, the rules were revised to protect the organization and the established authority. Gradually the rules evolved a life of their own. Assumed necessary for teaching the Gospel and protecting the interest of bishops and clergy, rules became sacred. The faithful went along, not noticing the ongoing subtle development. Probably, the bishops did not notice either, as they began to identify the rules with the Gospel. In much the same way that the visions of a political candidate can be subsumed by the opinions of his professional handlers, the rules took charge of the Gospel, to protect it by protecting the turf and authority of the bishops and clergy. In the final stage, the Gospel served to keep bishops and clergy in their estate by being the presumption behind the rules. The overthrow of organizational purpose by the rules was now complete, and the tail wagged the dog. Bishops and clergy controlled the people's cash. In Boston, the rules went further astray; the Archbishop alone controlled all the cash, as will be seen below.

It is important to note that the bishops were not bad guys out to take over the world. Rather, they suffered from an organizational pathology inherent in the dynamics of any organization. The rules, necessary to set up organizational structure, become judged by bureaucrats as sacred because they protect the bureaucrats from arbitrary decisions of superiors and others. Subordinates therefore defend rules as indispensable, even when they clash with institutional purpose. No organization in history has escaped this dynamic.

Down the road a few years, Vatican Council II, under the visionary auspices of John XXIII, achieved a remarkable accomplishment. It overcame this pathology. The assembled bishops inverted the pyramid structure of organization and the Church reverted to its original role as the Servant of the People. A servant, by definition, looks to others for direction.

My studies in Rome came to an abrupt end. As soon as I completed the course work in undergraduate theology, mother nature intervened. I came down with typhoid fever. It set the stage for me to return to the United States, where I began applying the rules in a parish setting.

—5—

Rules Applied

Recuperated and back in the States, a letter from Archbishop Cushing assigned me in September 1951 to St. Mary's Parish, Charlestown, Massachusetts. As with my duty on the *USS Philadelphia*, I lucked out. My seniors, uniformly friendly, gave helpful advice on pastoral techniques.

Once again, I arrived on duty with a trunkload of theory and a shortage of know-how. In contrast to my Navy experience, I arrived at parish duty with 30 years of exposure to the Church and its ways. I felt like a new teacher fresh from school about to enter the classroom to take charge of the learning. What gives me cold chills now is the total insensitivity with which I insisted on observance of Church rules, regardless of the human cost in terms of misery and suffering. I did my best to reaffirm the convictions of believers, bolster the wavering, and persuade the doubting, certain that Church rules came with the authority of God Almighty.

Monsignor Fred Allchin, the venerable pastor and decision-maker for parish affairs, proved a perfect gentleman, military in bearing, gruff-voiced but kindly, and a rock of common sense. He respected but did not fear any authority, civil or ecclesiastic. He could bend rules interfering with the best interests of his parishioners, like allowing solemn funeral ceremonies for their divorced and excommunicated parents. He kept close tabs on parish operations, but he delegated authority freely and without interference. He never saw his assistants as cheap help for tasks like counting the collection, driving him on errands, or babysitting the boss. A secure, well-balanced personality, he radiated strength and clarity of vision. Highly-respected by laity and clergy, he worked for religion to make sense out of life for both his parishioners and his assistants.

This big and busy parish served 10,000 members. It supported a grammar school with double grades, managed by 25 nuns. Another community of six nuns engaged in social work. The pastor and four full-time assistants lived in a large, four-story brick building on the corner of Monument Square, in the shadow of the Bunker Hill Monument. A full-time cook and a housekeeper, both of whom lived on the top floor, ran rectory logistics.

Down the hill stood the block-long granite and stained glass edifice of St. Mary's, with upper and lower churches. Its magnitude testified to the incredible generosity of the immigrants who paid for it out of scanty wages as laborers, clerks, and maids. Many of their descendants still lived in the parish, with the same strong faith but improved job status.

The Charlestown Navy Yard bounded one edge of the parish. The yard and neighboring docks gave employment to many parishioners. Main Street sported more barrooms per linear foot than I saw in any port, with the possible exception of Straight Street in Malta. Charlestown served also as a bedroom community for the labor force in Boston. Politically active, it supplied a continuing stream of talent for state and city governments, as well as for business and the professions. Bounded by water on three sides and connected to downtown Boston by two bridges, Charlestown instilled its population with local identity and pride, even after transfer to the suburbs. Grandparents generally stayed put, and their affluent offspring brought the grandchildren to visit. Elevated trains, on rails 20 feet in the air, prevented all conversation as they rattled and rumbled above Main Street. Grandchildren staying overnight with grandparents routinely could not sleep, to the amazement of their parents who heard not one train all night long.

Most of the citizens boasted of Irish Roman Catholic blood. When the pastor announced the news of a new assistant by the name of Father Schlichte, a very audible groan went through the big church. He told parishioners not to worry. "His mother's name was Muldoon." Sure enough, more than one caller asked at the rectory for the priest whose mother's name was Muldoon.

In a parish of such size and complexity, several funerals weekly complicated the scheduling of Masses on weekdays. A rotation plan set our turns at daily Masses, early and late in the lower church and early in both convents. The rotation got overruled by the funerals. We never knew our assignments until late the night before. The pastor posted them on a clip board at the head of the back stairs. A surprising fact accounted for this late posting. He never knew what state of sobriety to expect in the ranks of his assistants.

Archbishop Cushing had discovered long ago the pastor's ability to manage alcoholic priests, as well as the tolerance of the parishioners. After years of such extra duty, the pastor asked the Archbishop to clean out the house. I arrived as part of the new and sober crew. Comments I heard from parishioners all showed sympathetic understanding for my predecessors. Respect for clergy and religious convictions ran so deep as to create clear distinctions between a human affliction and the priest.

My discovery of alcoholism in the ranks of the clergy came as an unexpected and hitherto unconsidered eventuality. I never thought the grand theme of making sense out of life and death could lose its glamour. However, the work of a parish assistant, when constrained to institutional rule-keeping, can become mechanical and boring. The administration of sacraments can become a monotonous repetition of a ritual read verbatim from a book of formulas. The need to repeat the same lines to one person after another in the dead language of Latin could dull the edge of the dynamics and reduce the ritual to magic mumblings; although, for individual faithful, the strange, unintelligible sounds spoken by a specially-clothed minister might have added awe and mystique to the liturgy. The unrelieved tedium of the assistant's daily routine, coupled with the impossibility of independent decision-making, regardless of training, experience, or intelligence, easily led to lack of challenge, boredom, despondency, and closet alcoholism. Not many pastors possessed Monsignor Allchin's personality, and very few followed his management style. The system did not call for it.

Assistant pastors lived by and preached the rules. Only pastors made decisions about parish matters. Canon law said that pastors personally owned the income generated in a parish. Local statute set a monthly stipend for assistants. No preparation other than longevity qualified pastors for their job. Consequently, most of them did not allow any action they did not see other pastors doing. The whole organization ran by rules. At the bottom stood the basic motivator of fear. Pastors feared higher-ups and hell. The faithful feared pastors and hell. My great respect for Monsignor Allchin came from his freedom from fear. Reason dictated his decisions, based on the pastoral needs of his parishioners. He overruled me once. He entered the dining room and found me eating breakfast at 11:00 am. I had said the early parish Mass and then delivered Communion to shut-ins. From henceforth, he said, eat breakfast first.

It would be a mistake to characterize the majority of clergy as alcoholics. Most, of course, were sober. The ones who drank excessively had a disease which resulted from an intractable problem. "They do not have enough to do," said the by-then Cardinal Cushing when we reviewed this problem years later. In his study one Saturday afternoon, he looked up from his desk, glanced out the window at the rain and asked what I thought the rest of the clergy did. In reality I thought they watched football on TV or took siestas, but I knew he asked a rhetorical question, and so I gave a pious reply. I said they were probably preparing their sermons for Sunday. "Are you kidding?" he sputtered. "You and I are probably the only two damn fools in the entire Archdiocese who are working."

He often expressed concern at the lack of outlets for the abundant talent in the ranks of the clergy. His failure to find outlets stemmed from his control by procedural rules and his real fear of risking the wrath of Rome. I saw the basic problem as organizational. Arbitrary rules set up relationships which forced clergy to spend their most productive and energetic years in servitude to a pastor, who alone made decisions. Worse, the only preparation given this pastor came from a lifetime of seeking permission from a string of other pastors. The rules operated to hinder meaningful deployment of ministerial talent.

Why not cut the pie into smaller pieces? Make every ordained priest a pastor. Further, the job description should specify a leadership role for peace and justice, best defined as motivating people to respond to the needs of others, as well as administration of sacraments. The lack of challenge and decision-making authority in the lifestyle of parish assistants occupied much of my thoughts years later when I interviewed candidates for Pope John Seminary, all of whom demonstrated success at some secular occupation. Unless they saw their priestly work as including leadership for peace and justice, I worried that they faced a future as altar boys able to administer sacraments. I routinely asked why applicants wanted to enter the seminary. I always advised them we could teach administration of sacraments in less than one week. Hence, why spend four years in the seminary? I looked for some sense of a role as an advocate for peace and justice.

No church consensus existed on the job description for a priest, unbelievable as that may sound. I once asked a meeting of seminary rectors, deans of study, and spiritual directors gathered from the northeastern region of the United States, to define the product we produced. Hours later, the meeting broke up in chaos. Two threads ran through the discussions. One school held the priest in the sanctuary as administrator of sacraments. The other put him on the street as a motivator for people to lead selfless lives. One side saw the other as Merlin the Magician. The other saw priests reduced to secular status as social workers. I held out for both, convinced such a dual response gave challenge and a sense of accomplishment to the talents lying fallow in Roman Catholic clergy ranks.

Today I see this ambivalence about the function of clergy as another indicator of the takeover by the rules. The advocates for the social worker function held in mind the Gospel mission to respond to the needs of neighbors. The Merlin the Magician advocates held in mind observance of church rules, assuming observance of rules safeguarded the Gospel through scrupulously careful administration of the sacraments.

For the first year at least, I enjoyed my work in St. Mary's with the enthusiasm of a kid let out of school. From an organizational point of view, the Roman Catholic Church in the 50s lived in a Golden Age. The entire system marched to a single drummer. Iron discipline held sway over religious orders and clergy. Canon law with its catalogue of rules got the same reverence as the Ten Commandments. I too lived this dedicated promotion of the rules. I cajoled or scared many into conformity with canon law's dictates for marriage. The laity never questioned. Money poured in. Membership increased steadily. Archbishop Cushing made the Boston papers regularly with news of new schools, hospitals, and churches. Boston's seminary ordained an average of 40 new priests annually. Parochial schools enjoyed a seemingly-limitless supply of nuns. The Roman Catholic Church made the top echelon of well-managed international corporations. The ranking signaled triumph of bureaucratic rules. We thought it meant the Church and its leadership knew their stuff. In another corporate comparison, we, the field agents of the Church, functioned as order-takers for the established package. The product created its own demand in the United States, like a self-fueling industry.

Today, my wife and I live one street away from St. Mary's church. It is a sad sight bespeaking massive emptiness, as evidenced by its locked doors. The upstairs church, with its splendid stained glass windows and grand organ, gets rare use. The red brick grammar school across the street is closed and converted to housing. Both convents up the hill are empty of nuns and turned into private residences. The rules have worked their havoc.

Back in the early 50s, when all went by the rules, meals in the rectory went by the book. The large dining room contained a wall-length picture window overlooking the street leading to the church down the hill. The cook prepared meals downstairs on the ground floor, and the maid served them. We sat in seniority by date of ordination, not unlike in the ward room on the *Philadelphia*, where we sat in seniority by date of commission. The pastor carved and always asked our preferences. We wore either a cassock or black suit with Roman collar, except for the hottest days of summer when custom permitted shirt sleeves. Despite sharp differences in personality, conversation was kept at a polite level. Food, good, plentiful and well-prepared, came without alcoholic beverages. All Boston newspapers arrived each morning on the built-in bench under the long window. After lunch and supper, we assembled in the pastor's study. He smoked a cigar and discussed administrative details.

Sunday was the most attractive day of the week. Heavy attendance at Masses in the upper and lower churches brought the parish to life. The mountain of Sunday papers sold from the sidewalk in front of the church gave a good index of the traffic. Nowadays there is not a newshawk in sight.

I enjoyed preaching. I tried to give a return for the energy people expended in showing up. I worked hard at all my sermons. For one entire year I saved a copy of every one, thinking on the next annual cycle I could replay them. After the first year rolled around, I retrieved one of my past gems. It dismayed me to read such drivel. I reached all the way into the back end of the big bottom drawer of the desk, scooped the entire collection out, and dumped it into the wastebasket.

During this period, I unconsciously gained better insight into the discrepancies between the theory and practice of religion. In a parish of 10,000 people, I could not avoid improving my understanding of what it took to make sense out of life. Initially, I tried to demonstrate church dogmas as timeless and applicable to all situations. My personal evolution took me away from dogmas towards values, searching for ways to integrate service for others into the dynamics of modern living.

At an annual door-to-door parish census, the assistants counted heads and asked whether individuals had performed their Easter duty. This last meant receiving the Eucharist once a year, during the Easter season. Canon law required it. Failure to do so generally indicated underlying problems with either marriage or morality laws, suggesting that the individual was in a state of mortal sin and unable to receive Communion. The four assistant pastors each took one-fourth of the parish. We rotated our assignments annually. Problems with rules of canon law and daily living unearthed during the census set the agenda for our pastoral duties.

The census cards went to a central file. Whenever a call came to arrange funeral services, we first checked the census card. Was this a person in good standing and how much did the family give in the annual collection? Canon law forbade church funerals for the excommunicated, but the pastor never denied a request. He wanted to know about the contribution to the annual collection. If he thought it less than proper, he sent one of us to the wake, instead of going himself to offer condolences and say the rosary prior to the church services.

Whenever canon law said the pastor should deny funeral services, he assigned himself to conduct them. In his mind, these ceremonies benefitted the living. He gave a rare example of courageous independence. Absolutely loyal to the church, he followed the judgment of his pastoral conscience on behalf of his people. Rule enforcers in the chancery office never challenged him. He held strong cards. He suffered through a string of alcoholic assistants, which made the Archbishop beholden to him. He also organized the most massive display of Roman Catholicism ever seen in Boston, the Holy Name Parade. In it, men from parishes marched 25 abreast for over six hours. Furthermore, he ranked among the oldest priests in Boston.

Group meetings and premarital paperwork took up my evening hours. During the day, house calls, appointments at the rectory for private instructions in the rules, lectures in the grammar school, and discussion groups of teenagers kept me busy. Occasionally, I did counseling, for which I had received absolutely no preparation. I relied on old-fashioned horse sense to support the principles of moral theology. My seminary training in Rome dealt with the theology of orthodoxy. Not one lecture covered principles of social psychology or gave guidance for handling such human problems as child abuse, racial prejudice, or alcoholism. Today, I see this gap in seminary education as another consequence of takeover by the rules.

The construct of rules stood there as the Golden Calf, an idol we served through unquestioning obedience. We thought observance of the rules resolved all issues, and the social work nuns merely added frosting to the cake. We lived and worked heedless of silent screams for help with basic human needs. Granted, the Church built orphanages, hospitals, and schools. But it did little about wife-beating. The only discrimination we were aware of was the discrimination directed against us: "Catholics and Jews need not apply." Counseling meant convincing people to observe the rules. Our therapy consisted of one rule: offer it up. Pain and suffering in this world earned eternal reward in the next. Our primary mission was to do two things: keep believers compliant and get more people into our salvation net. As for addiction to alcohol, we administered a pledge to avoid it. If your husband insisted on birth control, tolerate, but don't cooperate. One man told me I did not know what it took to sleep on the floor at night. If your invalid marriage can't be fixed up, and you must stay together for the sake of the kids, live as brother and sister. It all seemed so simple. Mesmerized by the veneer of surface appearances, we thought the Gospel well-served. Look at the crowded churches. We did not hear the silent screams. Real issues went to civil courts, probation officers, and social workers. At the time, I thought it strange that the social work nuns made no referrals to us. Now, I understand why.

When I eventually could do something about seminary curriculum, Alcoholics Anonymous held meetings at Pope John Seminary and seminarians took courses in counseling. I wanted them better equipped than I to address the silent screams.

St. Mary's parish provided many people with what I had sensed in growing up: a refuge from the strain of the world about them. It also gave purpose to life. Tough as the grind became, it counted for eternity. The truly selfless offered their pain for the salvation of others. They united their suffering to that of the Son of God on the cross. Mixed in came a healthy dose of fear of divine wrath. It fed on itself, motivated by the rules of the Church as understood by them. Clergy arbitrated this fear and delivered salvation. For unsophisticated believers, this gave clergy a place of awe and honor. The more practical saw clergy as necessary instruments for the delivery of sacraments. We clergy believed all this.

However, rumblings began to stir our static base of the 50s. At the later masses on Sundays, a noticeable exodus started to take place before the concluding prayers. The pastor wanted it stopped. Words of advice from the pulpit and instructions from ushers availed little. One Sunday he suggested I stand at the back of church and direct the folks back to their pews. Once before I had faced a similar task on the *USS Philadelphia*. In the navy yard at quitting time, several hundred yard workmen rushed the gangway to leave the ship. We wanted them to line up so we could inspect whatever they took with them. Instructions to line up got no results. I jumped on top of a ventilator, pulled a pistol from my holster and waved it at them. We got an instant single file.

This time only my uniform helped as a persuader. Those who made the move to leave saw me and stayed put, except one young man.

"Where are you going?" I demanded.

"None of your business," he replied.

If he had passed close enough, I would have slugged him. For the first time in my life, someone defied my authority. Worse than irritated, I knew I could do nothing about it. At lunch, my associates reacted with glee at my predicament. Not so the pastor. He thought it not the least bit funny and said he would take care of it in his own way.

The young man lived in a house along the route we walked to the church. In the past, we had always exchanged pleasantries with people in the yard. The pastor decided not to speak to anyone in this yard on his trips up and down the hill to the church. Soon the young lad came to see me. "I apologize for my behavior," he said. "Now get the pastor to start talking to my family." The parents had noticed the new behavior of the pastor, asked around, heard about the incident with me and sent their son to apologize. Parents then thought it important to maintain good relations with the clergy.

The young man however, signaled things to come. Automatic obedience to rules died soon after Monsignor Allchin, along with automatic deference to authority figures. This parish eventually saw parents publicly defy and decry the pastor as they protested against busing to integrate the public schools. By then, the young man's generation had come of age.

Two years into my parish duties, my life as a parish assistant came to an end when the purple kingdom of rulekeepers invited me to become a drillmaster at the North American College in Rome.

—6—

Rule Master in the Purple Kingdom

One evening I answered the phone in my room at St. Mary's and heard an unfamiliar voice on the other end of the line. The speaker, Bishop Martin J. O'Connor, the rector of the North American College in Rome, solemnly invited me to join the faculty of the College. He explained that Monsignor Burns, the vice rector in charge of student affairs, needed an assistant. Both men had held their respective positions during my student days. O'Connor, correctly predicting that enrollment would soon double to 300, knew he needed to recruit more staff, especially since the College was also increasing its physical plant and had a new facility nearing completion.

O'Connor, tall and amply built, liked to eat. He had grown up in a Scranton, Pennsylvania hotel which his father managed. As a seminarian, he had attended the North American College, spending his summers in Switzerland with two maiden aunts who had sent him to riding school. In Scranton, he had gained notoriety as a pastor for the elegant table he provided. He thought his special mission in the Church charged him to educate others in gracious dining and papal protocol. Formal in the extreme, he was characterized by clergy pundits as a solemn procession of one. Ever conscious of his episcopal rank, he tended to frequent monologues. On the other hand, whenever he overcame his fear of making the wrong impression, he carried on interesting conversation, showed a good sense of humor and, surprisingly, demonstrated common sense.

Monsignor Burns, his vice rector, came from Rochester, New York. Of average height and slender build, he took himself seriously. Fastidious in dress and stubborn as a mule, he lived a life ruled by a schedule of his own making. Strict about College rules, he sought to revive student traditions from pre-World War II. During my student days, he had observed me handing mail to students. "Stand on the bench and toss it over their heads, the way we used to," he directed.

At the time I received the phone call inviting me to join the College staff, I was generally aware of each man's limitations and thought they both possessed dangerous traits which could make my life difficult. On the other hand, Rome was the residence of the Pope and the international headquarters of the Church. Besides, the work of seminary administration in Rome would offer welcome relief from my routine at St. Mary's. Although I thought my parish work was valuable, my tasks were beginning to seem repetitive and mechanical. On balance, the offer sounded attractive, like Navy orders to the Pentagon.

I decided to accept O'Connor's invitation. He asked Archbishop Cushing for my release, which was readily granted. With a certain sense of relief I prepared for Rome. Bishop O'Connor sent me to call on each of the four American cardinals and the Apostolic Delegate in Washington, D.C., the Pope's official link to the American bishops. O'Connor thought it politically important for me to be a known quantity. I looked on the visits as courtesy calls on admirals. Although I was now entering the ecclesiastical fast track, the Church did not undertake to pay my expenses, and my meager savings took a beating.

I booked passage on the *Andrea Doria*, tourist class. Claire Booth Luce booked the same ship, en route to Rome as the U.S. Ambassador to Italy. She invited me to tea. We exchanged thoughts on assorted topics. She complained about the impracticality of some monks to whom she had given an estate planted with expensive and very marketable orchids. The monks had plowed the orchids under to plant wheat, explaining to her that they had always planted wheat. Obviously, the monks, entrapped by rules, suffered a trained incapacity to think critically.

So did I. My behavior mirrored that of the monks. I assumed I lived as a free agent. Yet my behavior was governed by my firm, unproven conviction of the rightness of church rules. With this mind set, I took up my new duties.

Arriving in Rome, I immediately encountered the rigor of the ecclesiastical dress code. Late at night, I stopped at Dick Burns' quarters, dressed in trousers and white shirt. Instead of being handed an expected scotch on the rocks, I received a lecture on proper dress whenever outside my rooms and when receiving students. Cassock and collar were to be worn, with the addition of a long black coat and wide brim clerical hat whenever outdoors. I now faced the strictest dress code yet. Even in the middle of tropical summers, I sat through interminably long meals, cassock and collar buttoned tight around the neck despite the streams of perspiration running down my back.

College rules dealt with in-house behavior and local customs, all flavored by the personal prejudices of Burns and O'Connor. To instill his philosophy of proper social deportment, O'Connor continually lectured Burns and me. Appearances and public impressions made up his golden themes. He rarely contacted students directly. Reviewing the guest register one day, he saw a name he did not recognize. Informed it belonged to a student, he sent for him to explain "That register is for people, not students."

In Monsignor Burns, Bishop O'Connor found a like-minded lieutenant for strictness in matters of dress code, liturgical ceremonies, and sensitivity to Roman culture. Burns insisted that Roman culture required an appreciation for the baroque, a challenge for students who lived in the era of the atomic bomb. More seriously, Burns and O'Connor both demanded that training in Rome instill personal loyalty to the Pope.

Burns ran his side of the College for the sake of the old rules. This approach sometimes brought him into conflict with O'Connor, who approved only those old college traditions in tune with his ideas of proper social deportment. He wanted none of the schoolboy antics of the past. In particular, he did not want students up all night in bull sessions after lights out, and he did not want students in taverns instead of sightseeing, two of the traditions in pre-World War II days. Burns was caught between obedience to the boss and loyalty to the old traditions. He tried to straddle both by advocating privately for the old while lecturing formally against those disapproved by

O'Connor. He even prowled the corridors at night in search of clandestine activity. At the Naval Academy, officers of the watch prowled about in search of rule violations, but they had never advocated for the violations beforehand. Burns' excessive strictness and his dual standard eventually resulted in his dismissal by O'Connor.

When students violated rules, they were denied permission to leave the College on Thursdays, days without classes. The Thursday liberty allowed students to substitute black cassock for the college uniform, which freed them to enter stores, restaurants, or taverns. At the Naval Academy, clearly-defined procedures existed for hearings, punishment, and appeals. At the College, Burns set himself up as the whole show: rulemaker, law enforcer, prosecutor, judge, and jury. Such autocratic arbitrariness fit the church model of leadership. Burns' behavior typified that of a bishop in his own fiefdom.

Burns promoted military precision in liturgical functions. The practice in Rome, on the other hand, tended to improvisation. The person in charge of all papal ceremonies, Monsignor Dante, told us our students certainly conducted ceremonies well. "But," he added, "you have to admit they cannot improvise the way the Romans can." We took this remark as a facetious commentary on Italian lack of discipline. As I watched Dante over the years, I understood better. He tried to tell us to emphasize principles, rather than memorize rules.

For all his starchiness, Burns liked to play golf and introduced me to the course in Rome. One of his ground rules was to hide the fact that we indulged in such frivolity as golf. We set out for the course dressed in a black cassock, buttoned from head to toe, the cuffs of our golfing slacks tucked under our long black stockings, all of it covered by an equally long black coat, topped off by a broad-brimmed black beaver hat. To all the world, it looked as though we were heading for the funeral of some crown prince. Upon arriving at the club house, we stored the big hat on top of the locker, removed the coat and cassock, pulled the slacks out from underneath the long black stockings, which we removed, and put on golf socks and shoes. After we finished playing, we scrambled to reverse the process and rush back through the city to beat the students to the noon meal. Eventually, I found other clergy golfers from other institutions with a more sane approach and joined them. We stayed at the club house for lunch and even took showers.

In the late summer of 1953, preparations to formally open the new college building received a jolt. Pope Pius XII startled Rome with his decision to personally inaugurate the new seminary building of the North American College. It meant a break with the longstanding tradition of papal self-confinement to Vatican City.

The Pope's announcement shifted planning to papal masters of ceremonies, monsignors all. A monsignor is an honorary title. It carries no unique powers, but it does allow purple trimming on the cassock. We faced one special problem. Where to place the students? An army of dignitaries would more than fill the chapel. We suggested that students line the corridor the Pope would pass through en route to the chapel. At first, the papal masters of ceremonies objected. As products of Italian seminaries, they fully expected our students to break ranks, create a mob scene, and force the papal police to clear a path for Pius XII. This expectation probably resulted from the fact that in Italian seminaries, students entered in the fifth grade. Knowing the maturity of our students, we persuaded the monsignors to gamble on our seminarians' self-discipline.

As matters turned out, a relaxed and smiling Pius XII passed easily through the wide corridor of applauding students. When he entered the chapel jammed with purple robes and realized the exclusion of the students, he gave directions for them to follow him up the center aisle, where they remained for the ceremony.

Pius XII left the College immediately after he met individual members of the hierarchy. Not so with the later visit of Pope John XXIII, who came to the College in 1959 to celebrate its 100th anniversary. When those ceremonies were over, John XXIII toured the building and became separated from everyone when an elevator door closed, leaving him alone inside. An astonished cleric on the fifth floor gasped as the elevator doors opened. There stood the Pope. "I want to go to the roof to see the view." Up the two of them went, while the cleric held his hat over his cigar. Meanwhile, papal functionaries, Vatican police, and assorted ecclesiastics scrambled up six flights of marble stairs in frantic search for the Pope who broke all the rules.

—7—

Life in the Purple Kingdom

Bishop O'Connor's adherence to rules of the ecclesiastical bureaucracy knew no limits. His portly size added to his pontifical aura. During liturgical ceremonies, most bishops placed their miters on their heads and removed them unaided. However, the strictly proper method called for an attendant to do this. On one occasion, a nervous student placed the miter backwards on O'Connor's head. The two streamers on the back of the miter, intended to fall onto his shoulders, drooped over both eyes and hid his face. He looked mighty silly but sat there unmoving. A master of ceremonies crossed the sanctuary, removed the miter, and placed it properly.

O'Connor, determined to have the best, lacked the access to funds enjoyed by the bishop of a diocese. He compensated himself with perks which he made part of the operating budget. Cars and drivers, for example, were an important part of Roman ecclesiastical culture. The top of the line called for a Vatican uniformed full-time chauffeur and Vatican City plates on a four-door foreign-made car. A four-door Ford would qualify, so long as it was black with curtains on the back window. But no matter how hard he tried, O'Connor never succeeded in wrangling Vatican City plates for his four-door Mercedes.

Anyone of stature in the ecclesiastical world received the service of drivers. But while College faculty shared one non-uniformed driver, O'Connor demanded the service of a Vatican uniformed chauffeur, all to himself. Indeed, no matter how justifiable the reason, none of us was ever granted permission to use O'Connor's chauffeur or his College car. Vatican City chauffeurs performed a wide variety of useful services in addition to driving. They knew all of the latest gossip. They passed messages from their bosses to other heavyweights in the system without the bother of formal communications. For ladder climbers, they helped make or break deals by the words they spread on their network to their respective bosses.

Bishop O'Connor's need for visible signs of his stature found its fullest expression in the furnishings of the North American College, where he presided over an extremely formal and very large reception room called the Red Room. Off-limits to students, faculty and guests entered the Red Room through a corridor carpeted with a long red oriental rug and flanked by narrow mahogany tables. Once in the reception room, the purplish-red color scheme was carried through with floor-to-ceiling velvet window drapes and rosy marble columns, accented by red leather chairs with companion couches on oriental rugs in three large seating areas. Under an enormous crystal chandelier in the middle stood a round mahogany table. A floor-to-ceiling picture window on one side looked onto a long sloping driveway bordered by rolling lawns, lined on both sides by magnificent umbrella pines. The window framed the dome of St. Peter's in the background. In a city where perks defined status, the room ranked second to none.

The Red Room set the stage for entrance to the formal dining room, accessed through a foyer which displayed the seating plan when the number of guests warranted. The linen-covered dining table always displayed a centerpiece of fresh flowers. The seating arrangement always placed the Bishop in the middle of the row of mahogany chairs, facing a mahogany serving table which ran the length of the wall. The positioning gave O'Connor a commanding view of the service, as well as eye contact with the waiters. Waiters wore black shoes, trousers, and ties, with white shirts, jackets, and gloves. The ranking guest sat opposite O'Connor. Silver service and china displayed the College seal. Crystal goblets for water and wine accompanied the meals. A champagne glass signaled special visitors. More important visitors called for French champagne throughout the meal and menus printed with an appropriate dedication. O'Connor's gesture of frivolity was to pass around the printed menus for everyone to sign and take home as a souvenir. Unlike any other ecclesiastical institution in Rome, silver finger bowls arrived at each meal.

To support the demands of such an elegant table required domestic, kitchen, and supply staff. The sister superior of the community of 15 nuns managed these services. Nuns worked in the kitchen and laundry. They also took care of faculty rooms and did the purchasing of food. A dozen young laywomen helped. They lived in the convent on the grounds. Their families had entrusted them to the nuns, hoping they might safely make their way in the big city, or perhaps join the convent. A group of 15 young lads from the countryside cleaned the building and maintained the services for the student dining room. They lived in a dormitory, next to the garage, under the watchful eye of the sister superior. They were allowed off the grounds for only a few hours each week. A chief petty officer-type bossed them. Fresh from the farm and with a fourth grade education, it was challenging to prepare them for service in the faculty dining room.

Real pathos accompanied the elegant faculty dining. Many of the nuns and domestics came from dire poverty in which their families still lived. The faculty driver told me his standard lunch growing up consisted of a slice of bread with a dash of olive oil. Many of the nuns never ate candy, saving it instead to mail back to their families.

Knowledge of these backgrounds made me uncomfortable. I also disliked spending donated funds for niceties in dining. At one point, in charge of finances, I engaged in serious argument with O'Connor about our expenditures. Like most purple kingdom types, he believed upkeep of appearances was essential for the Gospel mission. I pushed for a rationale. He responded with the weakest form of argument, asserting, "Because I said so." Unfortunately, such authoritarianism was common in the purple kingdom, and I myself invoked it.

A more radical question concerned the use of the nuns for domestic services. By using nuns as housekeepers, the College bypassed the local labor market. These young women entered the convent in Switzerland to become members of the teaching profession. They ended up doing maid services for the College. They never complained. Obedience to the rules came before personal choice. And the first rule said they must respond to the decisions of the official Church.

None of us ever took issue with the party line and very few visitors did. Joe Kennedy, father of the well-known Boston political family, was an exception to this general rule. When O'Connor exceeded Kennedy's tolerance for pomposity, he bluntly told O'Connor, "Don't be such an ass." Kennedy had been annoyed by O'Connor's attempt to defend a then-prevalent attitude within the purple kingdom: ecclesiastical bureaucrats wanted to avoid the test of a Roman Catholic running for president of the United States. They reached their opinion based on fear, rather than reason and research. Above all else, they did not wish to risk losing status as Catholic dignitaries. Joe Kennedy once told me only two bishops in the United States made any sense, Spellman in New York and Cushing in Boston.

The Thursday noon meal provided the only sure relief from O'Connor's pontificating. Five American Jesuits, stationed in Rome, ate lunch with the faculty. On that day they did a morning stint at confessions and counseling of our nearly 300 students. The unfailing presence of Father Vincent McCormick, S.J., kept O'Connor in check. Father McCormick was held in extremely high esteem by ecclesiastical Rome. His primary duty as the American Assistant to the General of the Jesuits made him the boss of all the Jesuits in the United States. He enjoyed also the special confidence of Pope Pius XII, who consulted with him by telephone.

When I first came to the North American College as a seminarian, Father McCormick recalled my visit to him during WWII in the company of our ship's chaplain, Dan Burke, a Jesuit priest from New York. We became very good friends. He personally taught me how to say Mass. Later, as a faculty member, I turned to him for advice and counsel, especially about my behavior toward Bishop O'Connor.

Torn between obedience to the boss and common sense, I was in a constant dilemma with respect to O'Connor's never-ending demands for attention. McCormick advised me to confront O'Connor after one of his tantrums about my unavailability for his phone calls. I did, asking him whether he wished me to resign and return to Boston. He preferred for me to remain at the College.

One Thursday summer afternoon, as I chauffeured McCormick back to the Jesuit summer villa after an extended stay at the College, he gave me an insight into his personal character. "They say I am mellowing," he said and continued, "Do you know what that means? Either I am slipping now, or I did not do such a good job before." Soon thereafter, he returned to the ranks in a Jesuit community in New York.

About the time that Father McCormick was preparing to return to the United States, a surprising challenge to the purple kingdom brewed within its own ranks. It came from one of its key players, Archbishop Vagnozzi, appointed by Pope John XXIII to replace Cicognani as Apostolic Delegate to the United States, the Pope's official link with the bishops. Vagnozzi took up residence at the College just before assuming his duties in the USA. He preferred theological speculation to idle chit-chat. He instigated serious discussions, hitherto unheard of during our mealtimes. O'Connor sat uneasy, unable to direct the table talk of a senior officer whom he thought displayed none of the qualities appropriate for true kingdom dwellers. Besides, O'Connor's main reading diet consisted of the Saturday Evening Post. He became furious when Vagnozzi proposed the idea that no theological difference existed between a bishop and a priest. Too timorous to argue, he asked me later how could a man, about to give orders to all the bishops in the United States, make such a case? O'Connor left for the Excelsior Hotel in Naples with his Vatican uniformed full-time chauffeur. There, devastated, he took bed rest.

O'Connor got back at the radical. Vagnozzi came down with a high fever and retired to his room. For several days we managed his visitors. O'Connor got wind of it in Naples and headed for the College. "Don't you know this man has a bad heart? He has got to get out of here. We cannot afford to have him die on our hands."

So much for the care of the sick. Sure enough, O'Connor talked Vagnozzi into an ambulance ride to the hospital, where he recovered in short order. Two visiting United States cardinals had previously died at the North American College, Mooney and Stritch. Students nicknamed the College Marty's Mortuary. I doubt O'Connor picked up the tag line based on his first name, but fear of that reputation clearly motivated him to get Vagnozzi to the hospital.

All this happened just prior to Vatican Council II. The faithful generally saw the purple kingdom of ecclesiastical bureaucrats as the Kingdom of God on earth. I, too, separated a man with his foibles from the office he held, as did the parishioners at St. Mary's in Charlestown, Massachusetts. They separated the man with his alcohol problem from the priest who delivered salvation. This rationalizing made it difficult to know the emperor was wearing no clothes.

Money ran the engines of the purple kingdom. Without money, there could be no game. In Boston, during the late 60s after Vatican II, I outlined a vision of organized religion for several hundred teachers of religion. A question came from the floor.

"All you say sounds wonderful. But, in the ranks of parish life we are helpless, stuck with whatever the pastor and bishops decide to do. How can we bring about change?"

"You can get instant change," I replied. "When the basket passes in front of you on Sunday, instead of cash, drop in a note: 'When you guys get with it, this will turn to green.'"

Many money-raising strategies existed. Just before I left St. Mary's, Cushing had completed his takeover of all the cash in the Archdiocese. He incorporated the Roman Catholic Archdiocese of Boston as a civil corporation sole, a legal device which gave the Archbishop title to all the assets of the Archdiocese. Pastors of parishes became attorneys for the corporation. Cushing wasn't interested in the real property: the buildings, land, or equipment. He wanted the bank accounts, which he scooped. Pastors hitherto accustomed to uncontrolled income suddenly went on salary. By taking title to all assets, Cushing clearly violated canon law which gave pastors title to all parish income as a personal benefice. However, Boston clergy, disciplined to take orders, made no outcry. Knowing this history, I never sympathized with Cushing's failure to apply the same courage to effect needed changes in the job description of the clergy, which he acknowledged to be defective.

Access to sources of income was almost as useful as real cash. In O'Connor's case, an expense account under his control enabled him to purchase whatever he wanted. His one task was to get the budget approved by the American bishops, essentially from the American cardinals, all of whom sat on the College's Board of Trustees. Cushing, by contrast, had to collect his own money. He used to complain, "Sammy Stritch in Chicago has it easy. All he does is organize a couple dinners a year, invite a thousand gangsters at $1000 a head. Me, I have to run to bean suppers all year long and get a measly thousand bucks for a night's work."

At St. Mary's Parish, I learned the Archbishop of Boston could be had for any event. Like a singing telegram, he went anywhere invited, expecting a check for $1000. He worked at pleasing the crowd and saw himself as a showman. One evening in Boston, as I drove him home after a triumphal performance which left the crowd on its feet cheering loudly, he commented, "We let the folks forget their troubles for a little while."

At purple kingdom headquarters in Rome, fund-raisers used special twists of their own. They made the appointments of knights, dames, monsignors and bishops. They also arranged audiences with the Pope. Donations were expected for these services. There were several options for meeting the Pope. The most difficult to obtain was the strictly private audience, one-on-one at a desk. Then came various arrangements for shaking hands. People lined a corridor the Pope would be using en route to a large group, or they stood around three sides of reception rooms off the corridor, the number in each room according to the discretion of Vatican City functionaries. Another option placed people in the front line of a large group, to be greeted individually after the Pope addressed the group.

Felici, the official photographer, always stood with camera at the ready. He could make any picture look like a private meeting. He also disappeared on signal from papal functionaries, whenever it seemed politically inexpedient for a picture to be published. Those in the know saw his shoes under the drapery of a convenient window.

I, too, played in this game. Cushing sent me letters with advance warning of people coming to Rome. However, unless one had status as a friend of the Pope, the type and probability of an audience one could pull off diminished considerably. The faculty at the Graduate House of the North American College arranged papal audiences for visitors from the United States.

Any success came in proportion to their good rapport with the *Maestro di Camera*. Fortunately, another Bostonian on the faculty there, Frank O'Hare, managed to stay on good terms with this office, and he always delivered the requested audiences.

More lucrative than arranging papal audiences, the best Roman fund-raising technique was to sponsor a pious cause. Cardinal Spellman of New York sponsored playgrounds in Rome when he worked in the Secretary of State's office. Spellman really lucked out when his collaborator in the playground venture became Pope Pius XII. Aspirants to higher station in the kingdom contributed to these charitable projects in order to catch the attention of appropriate superiors. It could be very blatant. A pastor once asked me how he might contribute $1,000 to Cardinal Pizzardo's work with the seminaries in Italy. The Cardinal thereafter instructed me to say he could arrange for the good pastor to be made a monsignor.

The worst case I heard involved a Boston pastor who had amassed a fortune in real estate. When on-duty in the chancery office, he spent much of his time inspecting and buying up land ahead of developers. Cardinal Cushing told me the pastor had offered him one million dollars in return for nomination to bishop. Cushing turned him down.

In Rome during my tour, Monsignor Tardini ranked as the most notorious manipulator for a cause. He ran the Office of Secretary of State, which he had co-chaired with Monsignor Montini until Pius XII dismissed him. After Montini's dismissal, Tardini sat alone in a key seat of the empire. He took up the charitable cause of the Villa Nazareth, an orphanage on the outskirts of Rome. Aspirants to the purple and those seeking greener pastures beat a path to Tardini's door with cash for Villa Nazareth. Lacking cash, an aspirant could always arrange for visits to Tardini by affluent potential donors. Here, papal audiences entered the scene.

A personal meeting with the Pope generally commanded a visitor's interest. Tardini had the clout to put such a meeting on the Pope's schedule. The rest of us depended on the good will of the *Maestro di Camera,* the office which scheduled the Pope's appointments. What better way to impress an affluent parishioner than to suggest an introduction to the man who ran the office of Secretary of State and who could arrange a meeting with the Pope?

It was all so simple. On behalf of an affluent parishioner, a purple kingdom climber would write a letter to Tardini. Upon arrival in Rome, the tourist would call Tardini's office to make an appointment for a visit past the barrier of Swiss guards. After a brief exchange, Tardini would offer to arrange a special audience with the Pope because their mutual friend had recommended the visitor so highly. Of course, the conclusion of the conversation always would be, "By the way, you really ought to stop and see what great things are being done in Rome for orphans."

Villa Nazareth kept the sad-faced orphans and the script at the ready. Truly large benefactor prospects got accompanied to the Villa by Tardini himself. The papal audience over, picture with the Pope taken, the impressed tourists returned home and naturally reported their wonderful experience to the intermediary, who would immediately capitalize on his parishioner's euphoria and request a check for Villa Nazareth. The genius of this entire game, Tardini, sat at the intersection point of everybody's self-interest. The tourists got what they wanted, a handshake with the Pope and a picture to show their friends. The purple kingdom climber got what he wanted, a chance to be of service to a dispenser of the purple, and Tardini got what he wanted, a check. The reward to the kingdom climber remained hanging in the bight. It served as the carrot for another round and increased the quotient of expectation and hope in the purple kingdom.

Cardinal Spellman played with the same deck in New York. There, he dealt personally with the benefactors. To Rome, he simply sent notice and audiences got arranged. No other American ecclesiastic had the same amount of clout. He stands out as the only person I ever heard of who dined with Pius XII, albeit at a lower but adjoining table.

Spellman absolutely terrorized Bishop O'Connor, whom he routinely kept waiting for an hour at scheduled appointments. Spellman could not resist any opportunity to upset O'Connor. O'Connor's penchant for pomposity made matters worse. One day at lunch at the College, Spellman took a business card out of his pocket, scribbled some words on it and handed it to Joe

McGeough, a priest from New York working in the office of the Secretary of State. "Tell your boss to make you a monsignor." O'Connor sat there horrified at Spellman's cavalier approach to such an awesome matter as the awarding of the purple.

This kind of political maneuvering was to lead to the next step in my own career when in 1954, back in Boston, Archbishop Cushing held a very unusual audience. In the hospital, apparently terminally ill, he refused to sign a proffered document of resignation. His life hung by a thread, but he remained politically aware enough to know Cardinal Spellman wanted him out of office. Word on the grapevine said that Spellman intended to replace Cushing with O'Boyle, at that time Archbishop of Washington, D.C. In the gossip circuit, Cushing was being ranked as too loose a cannon on deck.

To the amazement of the medical world, Cushing recovered. Months later, when Dr. Charles Stanton visited Rome, I told him Cushing asked me to take good care of him because he owed him his life. He said Cushing had no medical right to be alive.

Cushing, a shrewd master of his own spoils system, realized that his own chancellor had followed Spellman's bidding by offering him the resignation paper while he was at death's door. Cushing fired the disloyal chancellor and cabled Monsignor Sennott, a Boston priest, to return immediately and take up duty as chancellor. At the time Sennott served as business manager of the North American College. O'Connor asked me to assume Sennott's duties. I did. It pleased me to get out from under the unreasonable reins of Burns. O'Connor's only directive was to make the dining room the equal of the best embassies in Rome.

The duties of business manager were right down my alley. They required little of the learning I'd spent six years to acquire in the seminary. Instead, I applied personnel policies and management skills I'd learned in the Navy. The Navy's training did the job; during my tenure as fiscal manager from 1954 to 1958, the College operated within its budget, and O'Connor got the service he desired in the dining room.

To accomplish these tasks, I enjoyed help not utilized by others. It came from the architect of the College, Count Galeazzi, a truly extraordinary and gracious man, who managed the financial and technical services for Vatican City. He met with Pope Pius XII weekly as part of a three-person kitchen cabinet, the other two being the Pope's housekeeper, Mother Pasqualina, and the Pope's nephew, Prince Pacelli. Galeazzi not only made innumerable visits to help me, but put the technical experts of Vatican City at my disposal, sending his personal bookkeeper over to help. He himself sat with the two clerks in my office and demonstrated how to organize a paper trail of cash flow.

Officially, Galeazzi served as the lay delegate to the Cardinals' Commission for Vatican City. He also held the title of Architect for the Sacred Apostolic Buildings. Through the Commission he controlled all the resources of Vatican City. During Galeazzi's tenure, Vatican City operated with positive cash flow, a novelty for it. Captains of industry and finance, such as Joe Kennedy, father of the future president, vied for Galeazzi's attention. Unequivocally committed to the best interests of the church, Galeazzi turned down a request from Coca Cola to be chairman of operations in Italy, but did accept the same proposal from RCA. As he explained to me, "Association with Coca Cola seemed too frivolous in light of my duties towards the Holy See."

He could manage money without being consumed by its pursuit. He gave up a road-building business because it simply made money. Instead, he took over problem-solving for both Vatican City and the Holy See. (Vatican City is the title for the civil state where the Pope resides, while the Holy See is the designation for the Pope as head of the Roman Catholic Church). An architect by profession, Galeazzi directed maintenance and repair of all properties owned by the Holy See. Despite his change in employment, his name made the annual listing of the 10 biggest taxpayers in Italy. As part of his management of Vatican City money, he founded and chaired the largest land and real estate holding corporation in Italy, the *Societa Immobiliare*. It eventually owned the Watergate Hotel in Washington, D.C. and similar properties around the world.

However, even Galeazzi got squeezed by politics in the purple kingdom. Pope John XXIII succeeded Pius XII and kept Galeazzi in office. When Paul VI took over after John XXIII, he replaced Galeazzi. Vengeance rather than politics explained this action. Prior to Paul VI being elected Pope by the College of Cardinals, he was known as Cardinal Montini, the Archbishop of Milano. He had become Archbishop of Milano after Pope Pius XII summarily dismissed him from the office of Secretary of State, which he had co-chaired with Monsignor Tardini. Mother Pasqualina explained to me that Galeazzi caught Montini red-handed, double-dealing with Pius XII. He had told the Pope one thing and done another. Conveniently, the Archdiocese of Milano opened at the time and Montini suddenly found himself appointed Archbishop of Milano. By a nice coincidence, this position carried with it the rank of cardinal. Montini merely waited until being so named.

With an eye toward the future, politically savvy Montini spent time making himself known to cardinals around the world. Out of the ranks of cardinals would come the future popes. To get elected pope, you needed only one thing: the votes of the cardinals. The voters, scattered around the world, hardly knew each other's names. A world-traveling candidate could fill in this void and become known. Very likely he could pick up enough swing votes to catch attention on the first round and win election on a subsequent one. Montini's strategy got him elected. It seems not to have been lost on the more aspiring in the ranks of the purple kingdom. The present Pope, John Paul II, did his share of world traveling as a Polish cardinal.

The unfortunate bank in Vatican City, from which the non-forgiving Paul VI ousted Count Galeazzi, became involved in criminal as well as financial irregularities. Ultimately it lost money on a grand scale. Paul VI placed it under the direction of Monsignor Marcinkus, bright, accommodating, a great golfer and thoroughly dedicated to the purple kingdom. However, neither his seminary training in Chicago nor his years of dedicated service in the office of the Secretary of State in Vatican City prepared him for the rapacious world of international finance, a world where Galeazzi ranked as an acknowledged ringmaster. Although lacking financial sophistication, Marcinkus obviously stood high in the opinion of Paul VI. During the Pope's travels, television watchers saw his big frame always within a few feet of the Pope. I ate breakfast with Marcinkus shortly after Paul

VI took office. "We certainly took care of your friend, Galeazzi," he commented.

He had to rue the day Galeazzi got sacked. Marcinkus' innocence became rapidly exploited by the barracudas of international finance. To escape arrest by the Italian police, he experienced life as a virtual prisoner in Vatican City.

As the business manager of the College, I reverted to Navy ways. I exercised relentless dedication to the rules. I behaved towards personnel and students as I did towards sailors on the *USS Philadelphia*, where I extracted proper performance but kept an eye on the welfare of the crew, like watching the chow line. Occasionally, on the *Philadelphia*, I relieved a timid sailor of his tray with gristle and watery vegetables, took it back to the serving line with the rhetorical question, "Would you eat this swill? Dump it and put food on that tray."

Now, in Rome, my language and tone softened, so I thought. But the same game continued. I concentrated on creating efficient and effective operations. I justified my behavior with the thought that I was helping improve the human condition more by training future religious leaders than by getting into the action myself.

However, even while dedicated to true purple kingdom behavior, I encountered and dimly sensed that authoritarian structures presented problems. I once noticed the globe from the ceiling light in a student's room sitting on a bookshelf. I saw an inevitable crash and directed the student to replace it. Instead of compliance, he asked for a reason.

"May I ask why?"

I saw obedience to authority flying out the window.

"Because I said so," I replied.

Entrenched in the purple kingdom operating principle that higher authority always knew best, I instinctively appealed to this principle and thought no reasons were necessary. Curiously, I struggled over my own differences with O'Connor at the time about his lavish dinners and felt that his authoritarian reasoning was unacceptable.

By his very question, the student challenged blind obedience, a hitherto unthinkable action on the part of seminarians. The incident stuck in my mind, but did not result in any immediate increase in my tolerance for seeming insubordination.

Many years later, this questioning of authority was to become a worldwide phenomenon within Roman Catholic circles. During Vatican II, purple kingdom types considered the challenges a malaise to be treated after the Council closed. However, at the time, I went along with this blind defense of authority.

Nonetheless, the day finally came when I privately applauded seminarians on strike. They were marching in protest against the rector of the Boston seminary, Larry Riley, an arch defender of the purple kingdom. He resisted the changes coming out of Vatican II, as any true kingdom keeper would. In this instance, he had refused to allow English in the liturgy. The exasperated students took matters into their own hands and paraded on strike around Cardinal Cushing's house. As the students knew, Rome had authorized seminary rectors to use English in the liturgy. Riley's intransigence typified the lack of vision, understanding, and tolerance inherent in the purple kingdom's self-appointed defense of self-defined orthodoxy. Riley became so upset by the students' strike that he resigned. The Cardinal accepted his resignation and made him a pastor. But the purple kingdom could not allow such dedication to the old rules go unrewarded. By way of encouragement for other system-keepers to hold ranks, Rome made Riley a bishop.

Unfortunately, Cushing never understood the purple kingdom. Instead, he developed an inferiority complex with regard to it and viewed its authority with fear. He suffered accordingly. His failure to be named a cardinal increased his already fearful attitude. He even feared O'Connor, to whom he generously released Boston priests for duty at the College and to whom he gave large cash donations.

Bad advice from those he presumed knowledgeable had caused him unfortunate experiences in Rome. He earned a reputation for mixing the wrong people at the wrong dinners. O'Connor told him he violated every protocol in the books. His social and political blunders looked so bad that it seemed that those responsible for orchestrating his trips to Rome were deliberately fouling him up. Bishop John Wright, later named Cardinal, and Monsignor Ed Murray, at one time the rector of the Boston seminary, got the credits for bungling the protocol. Both were former students at the North American College and had been much favored by Cushing's predecessor, Cardinal

O'Connell. Cushing, a product of local seminary training, saw Wright and Murray as mentors for protocol with Rome. I never determined whether they simply followed a seminarian's view of politics in Rome or tried deliberately to create sparks. Whatever the reason, in practice, Cushing got jolted by any contact with headquarters.

Bob Sennott, Cushing's new chancellor whom I replaced as business manager, came to Rome in the summer of 1954, along with Cushing and a large group of tourists. Sennott and I determined to keep that visit free from diplomatic blunders on Cushing's part. As events developed, Cushing put Pius XII on the defensive because the Pope himself made a blunder. The large pilgrimage group which Cushing brought to Rome that summer merited a special audience with Pius XII. The Pope walked into the room, went directly up to the Archbishop and said, "Tell me, how is Archbishop Cushing?"

"I am Cushing," replied the astonished Archbishop.

Undoubtedly, Pius XII had known of Cushing's ill health and Spellman's choice for a replacement. The Pope's gaffe was worsened by Cushing's knowledge of Spellman's plans and Cushing's determination to travel to Rome despite medical advice to the contrary. Cushing felt really crushed. That night, sitting next to him on a large sofa in the lobby of the Hotel Roma, I desperately groped for the words to help him over this shock. Monsignor Joe McGeough from the Secretary of State's Office arrived unexpectedly. He delivered to the Archbishop a huge silver medallion in a red velvet-lined box, a gesture of apology from the Pope.

Whether the papal blunder set ecclesiastical Rome in a mood to make amends, or Sennott and I arranged the correct events, or Cushing felt he had at last got Pius XII on the defensive, this visit ranked as a success on his part. As he boarded the train for Naples, he announced to assembled bystanders that the time had come to make me a monsignor. Further, he leaned over toward me and said I deserved a monthly check from him for all the errands I ran. He followed up on both counts, but changed his mind about the monthly check when Cardinal Spellman chose me as one of his two assistants at the Conclave to elect a new pope.

—8—

Rule Changes in the Air; John XXIII Elected Pope

Ecclesiastical Rome can be an impossible maze, or a very small town, depending on how one is perceived in relation to the Pope. A veritable army of clergy, clerks, janitors, guards, and chauffeurs watch the comings and goings, alert to catch the direction of the wind and regulate behavior accordingly. They thrive when they pick winners and stick with them. In my case, Galeazzi's obviously special treatment made the city a small town where I could get things done easily. At the Vatican customs office one day, the agent in charge started to make problems for me and abruptly stopped. Galeazzi, he said, had told them I determined the legitimacy of any import to the College.

One morning, the telephone in my bedroom rang before the alarm clock. Monsignor Dante's office, the Papal Master of Ceremonies, announced Pius XII had just died. Could I go to Castel Gandolfo, the papal summer residence, and stand watch at his bedside while civil and church dignitaries paid their last respects? The assignment called for the rank of papal chamberlain, or junior-grade monsignor, to which Archbishop Cushing recently had appointed me.

Vatican City cars delivered eight of us to the papal residence before 8:00 a.m. Swiss guards stationed along the main staircase to a reception area and along the following corridor showed the way to the Pope's bedroom. The body of Pius XII, clothed in a white cassock, was lying on a small four-posted bed. Four at a time, we stood at the corners of his bed while cardinals, ambassadors to the Holy See, and city of Rome dignitaries filed past. Not a member of his family or immediate staff could be seen. A very official atmosphere prevailed. The presence of four of us in red cassocks confirmed the official nature of the day. In the late afternoon, attendants transferred the body to a large hall. Seminarians relieved us, and local townspeople entered to walk past the bier. The next day, a solemn procession took place to St. Peter's, where Pius XII laid in state in front of the papal altar directly under the dome.

Immediately after the Pope's death, no single decision-maker existed. Officials whose job descriptions clearly called for certain functions, such as papal masters of ceremonies, made decisions which no one questioned. Those whose offices and authority depended on the will of the pontiff became conspicuous by their low profiles. The cardinals collectively ran the Church, each one cautious not to act individually. Cardinals stationed in Rome suddenly took on less autocratic personalities. One person generally stepped in when no decision-maker came forward, the papal photographer. Thanks to years spent watching papal functions, he knew exactly what to do. "At times like this," he said to me, "everybody is a little bit in charge." In the void surrounding the pope's death, we achieved a temporary sort of management by consensus in a world otherwise authoritarian.

Cardinals arrived from around the world. We ended up with two in residence at the North American College: Mooney from Detroit and McIntyre from Los Angeles. Spellman from New York took a suite at the Hotel Roma, but came to the College every noon for lunch. Bishop O'Connor thought three cardinals under foot a colossal burden. From my point of view, they proved less troublesome and more interesting than O'Connor's monotonous harangues in support of the purple kingdom. He caved in at the thought of 10 days with three cardinals in the house, went to the hospital for bed rest, and left the dignitaries in the hands of the faculty.

Mornings kept the cardinals at funeral ceremonies and committee meetings in connection with the upcoming Conclave, at which they would elect the next pope. Routinely, the three Cardinals were back at the College for lunch, which they ate with the faculty. Mooney and McIntyre generally ate supper with us, while Spellman operated from the Hotel Roma. At lunch, Spellman sat obediently at the table until Mooney, his senior, gave the signal to break.

On the day of the Conclave, Cardinal Mooney held forth as usual at lunch, looked at his watch, and announced time remained for a siesta before heading to Vatican City and the Conclave. The general exodus from the dining room scarcely ended when the phone rang. Mooney's secretary asked me to call the college doctor. We knew he might be victim of a heart attack and guessed the problem. The college doctor, already in special uniform to enter the Conclave as attending physician, thought we should call another doctor. I told him our sick cardinal might not last until the Conclave. He came at once. I escorted him to Mooney's room where McIntyre paced the floor at the foot of the bed, reading psalms. Obviously, the end had come, which the doctor confirmed.

Meanwhile Bishop O'Connor hotfooted it back to the College, fearful of unexpected consequences. He asked me to stick around until Mooney's body was shipped off to the States. However, I had an unexpected conflict. Because of a quirk in conclave rules, Spellman had nominated me as one of his two assistants. At the appointed hour, the entrances would be sealed shut, leaving only a turnstile open for written messages. Before I could leave the college, the authorities of Vatican City and the City of Rome had to give clearance to send the body of Cardinal Mooney to the States. I caught Count Galeazzi in his office at Vatican City. He came to the College, made some phone calls, and told me to leave the matter with him. I explained Galeazzi's offer, and O'Connor gave grudging consent for me to attend the Conclave, where I met Spellman and his secretary.

Each cardinal could bring two assistants, neither to rank above a papal chamberlain, a monsignor junior-grade. Spellman had planned to include a domestic prelate, which is a senior grade of monsignor. When the committee of cardinals charged with admissions told him to find a less senior substitute, Spellman chose me.

Spellman sat on the housing committee. We occupied half of a completely furnished apartment with two baths. The ecclesiastical occupant had gotten bumped because he happened to reside within the conclave area. Cardinal Pizzardo and his one lay assistant occupied one room each, as did Spellman and his secretary. I slept on a cot in the dining room and stocked the refrigerator with extras on the morning of the lock-up. We lived in relative luxury. I saw cardinals with quarters made by curtains at the ends of corridors and under stairways. All the cardinals ate meals at one oval table. The rest of us ate at long tables in a nearby room. After the second morning, Spellman announced he could take these cardinals at lunch and supper but not for breakfast. I then boiled the eggs.

Morning and afternoon each day, we escorted cardinals to their voting sessions in the Sistine Chapel, went sightseeing within the conclave area, and watched out windows for the smoke signal which told whether or not a ballot resulted in an election. We told Spellman nobody could tell whether the smoke came out black or white. He took it up with the attendants at the stove, and more readable signals were quickly produced.

The election of Cardinal Roncalli as Pope John XXIII produced surprises from the beginning. Clergy from the Secretary of State's Office broke the seals and entered the conclave area. Cardinal Tisserant, like a French field marshal, ordered them out and excommunicated for violating the Conclave. The new Pope suggested they leave, but they were not excommunicated, and he further suggested that the Conclave continue until after Mass the next morning.

John XXIII, meanwhile, sent word for some of his old cronies to come in for supper. Hitherto, the Pope dined alone. He gave us a signal: If a rule made no sense, it would be changed. A change in papal style was even more clearly signaled when the newly-elected John XXIII commented that he'd reached "the end of the road, but the top of the heap."

The Boston papers carried detailed reports of these events in Rome. Archbishop Cushing, one of the interested readers, soon wrote a letter to me and said that money was tight, and he could no longer send me the $100 monthly subsidy he had started after his successful visit to Rome. He made no mention of Cardinal Spellman, presumed to be the man behind the move to put O'Boyle in Cushing's office. To this day I suspect my loss of stipend came not from financial constraints but rather from my boss' pique at my presumed disloyalty in accompanying Cardinal Spellman to the Conclave.

Events in the offing were soon to change his mind and my mind and send shock waves throughout the purple kingdom.

—9—

Archbishop Cushing, Complex Showman

The new Pope John XXIII took a pastoral approach, much like Monsignor Allchin at St. Mary's in Charlestown. Focusing his attention on people, rather than on organizational structure, Pope John soon irritated cardinals stationed in Rome. At their regularly-scheduled audiences, he avoided discussing bureaucratic affairs. Instead, he directed conversation to domestic matters, like the health of the cook and new recipes. These top keepers of the kingdom moaned about their inability to get him down to what they considered serious business. At the time, I sympathized with them. In retrospect, given the Pope's plan to assemble a General Council to let in a bit of fresh air, I think John XXIII was trying to give the cardinals in Rome a message. "Quit tinkering with details, we are headed for a major overhaul."

For his first big event, he announced a Consistory, a ceremony to create new cardinals. The symbol of this highest ecclesiastical honor is an enormous red hat, much too big to wear. Its only use is to hang from the cathedral ceiling after its recipient dies. For years, Archbishop Cushing and the Archdiocese of Boston had languished under the illusion of missing something because Cushing hadn't made it to the rank of cardinal. Pius XII had kept him out of the club, presumably because of his maverick ways.

In terms of bureaucratic prestige and other purple kingdom values, Cushing missed out. But in Gospel values, like

Ben Adhem, he led the pack. He inspired his flock to help others in need. His measure of success could be gauged by his extensive financial support of worthy causes around the globe. When John XXIII announced the Consistory, Archbishop Cushing made the list of new cardinals.

Because Cushing had had a politically successful and smooth trip to Rome the previous summer, he expected a repeat performance for his red hat adventure. He gave Sennott and me his complete cooperation. He trusted us, a rare interlude in the life of a man who, I later discovered, had difficulty deciding on a course of action and sticking to it.

Three planeloads accompanied him for the ceremonies. Cushing and Sennott took up residence at the College. The entourage stayed in hotels. Sennott and I scheduled Cushing's every minute, to the eventual dismay of the camp followers. One of them complained to me he might just as well have stayed home and watched events on television. Their messages to Cushing fell on deaf ears. He stuck to the schedule as outlined.

Encouraged by the new Pope, extensive media coverage added a new dimension to the tranquil and controlled world of staid, ecclesiastical Rome. Cushing made good copy. He understood the value of publicity for his fund-raising. His cooperation with the secular press was unusual in the purple kingdom, whose bureaucrats usually avoided the uncontrolled media, asserting that appearance in the secular press was too worldly. However, I was in complete agreement with Cushing's penchant for publicity, and during this visit to Rome, I accommodated the needs of the press, arranging ringside space for them at events in the College and giving direct answers to their questions. O'Connor complained about this freedom for the press, but feared to offend Cushing. Many years later, when I was Rector of Pope John Seminary, openness to the press proved invaluable. Having had some experience with media relations, we were able to mount a campaign to expose the public to the ideas of Vatican II, ideas which the purple kingdom feared and did its best to suppress.

Cushing's red hat experiences earned rave reviews. He invited all the right people to the right dinners. The new Cardinal left Rome delighted with his outcome. He told me I deserved another promotion, this time to the rank of Domestic Prelate, or senior-grade monsignor. He also restored my monthly allocation, with a note in which he wrote that I met his ideal of what a secretary should be. My previously-perceived disloyalty became forgiven in a tangible way. Back in Boston, he announced a refreshed attitude towards the papacy, proclaiming to all that John XXIII was the only pope who ever understood him. True to his nature, he also told everyone he came back from Rome with a new hat, a bad cold, and empty pockets.

Shortly after Cushing returned to Boston, Mother Nature was again to intervene in my fate and provide occasion for a change in venue. I had been having bouts of fever for some time, which eventually culminated in pneumonia. The fevers got out of hand, and one night I awoke in a daze, surprised to find Mother Pasqualina on a chair next to my bed. She stayed with me until the ambulance arrived. Mother Pasqualina was a dedicated, talented woman. As the housekeeper for Pius XII, she had managed all domestic details in the papal household. She did duty also as a brainy member of the Pope's three-person kitchen cabinet. Since Pius XII continued the papal practice of self-inflicted exile within Vatican City to protest past behavior of the Italian Government, Pasqualina did the Pope's errands and delivered his personal messages around town. The sight of her, chauffeured in a four-door black car with curtains over the back window, stirred the imaginations of gossips in papal intrigue. After Pius XII's death, she took over as superior of the nuns at the North American College, where I worked with her daily and gained great respect for her abilities.

Mother Pasqualina came to the North American College because her community of nuns from Menzingen in Switzerland was already providing domestic services at the College. O'Connor, always alert to opportunities to build rapport with the papacy, had invited the nuns to come to the College while Pasqualina was working in the Vatican. His chief argument to them emphasized the advantages of a permanent base in Rome. When Pius XII died, Pasqualina replaced the nun in charge at the North American College. After only a few months, everyone praised Mother Pasqualina's pleasing personality, her concern for the well-being of all, and her ability to get things done.

Only O'Connor complained about her presence. The great of the world continued to call on her, without so much as a wave to him.

Mother Pasqualina visited me daily in the hospital. When I was discharged, she took a week's leave to supervise my recuperation at Count Galeazzi's villa in Circeo. After Circeo, I went to the United States to continue recuperating at my parents' home in Florida. When I had finally recovered, enroute back to Rome, I stopped at the Chancery Office in Boston before I scheduled a visit with Cardinal Cushing. "The Cardinal would like you to stay in Boston as vice chancellor," said Bob Sennott, the chancellor. This remark took me by surprise. Sooner or later, as part of my career development, such a move had appeared inevitable. Now, although I hadn't expected the offer at this time, it came as a welcome escape from an increasingly strained relationship with O'Connor.

Differences in style, personality, and outlook were leading to heightened conflicts with O'Connor. He particularly disliked the tendency of Galeazzi to seek me out for informal meetings, while limiting him to strictly formal occasions. We clashed also over the use of College funds. "Why can't you listen to others as you do to Father McCormick and Count Galeazzi?" was one of his not infrequent rhetorical questions. Further, I thought O'Connor made excessively self-centered demands on my time. Every time Cushing visited Rome, O'Connor became frustrated by my lack of availability for phone calls. The frosting went on the cake when producers of "Person to Person" put me on for half of the scenes with Charles Collingwood. They thought O'Connor too much to take for the whole show. He saw himself pushed into second-fiddle position, thanks to me. When I thought about returning to the North American College, I saw myself faced with interminable monologues about proper behavior in the purple kingdom, like "Will you please wear your hat square on your head?"

Sennott made it clear that both he and Cushing wanted me to work in Boston. I agreed, cabled the news to O'Connor, and asked him to ship my belongings to the Chancery in Boston. I then received a very formal letter from Cardinal Cushing, delegating me to act in his name for all matters not expressly reserved by law to him. I now sat with authority in the

Chancery Office, the executive office of the Cardinal. At the time I thought I would be doing meaningful work in the real world served by the church. Instead, I got an even heavier dose of the rules in the purple kingdom.

First of all, I experienced a surprising bit of political maneuvering that surrounded my appointment to the Chancery. One afternoon, Count Galeazzi telephoned from Rome. He read me part of a letter which Cardinal Cushing had written to Mother Pasqualina, saying that it broke his heart to see me give up such a great opportunity in Rome. Also, in the letter, Cushing said that I had asked to be transferred from Rome to Boston. This letter was my first exposure to Cardinal Cushing's tendency to play both sides of the street. Wanting me to stay on in Boston, but fearful of offending the powerful in Rome by ordering me stateside, Cushing made it appear that staying in Boston had been my idea.

Surprised by the letter, I told Galeazzi what had really happened and summarized the offer that Bob Sennott had made as I was enroute back to Rome. To clear up confusion, Galeazzi suggested I speak to the Cardinal directly to make certain I was carrying out his wishes and that there hadn't been any miscommunication between Sennott and me. I arranged to see the Cardinal.

"How's it going?" he asked from behind the desk in his study.

"Not too badly," I answered. "I talked to the folks in Rome. They hear I asked to be transferred to the Boston Chancery and that you think I am making a terrible mistake."

"Pay no attention to them, your place is here," Cushing continued. "I think you should stay here. If you want, I will give you a letter to that effect."

"I don't need the letter," I answered. "I just needed to make sure you really want me here and that there hadn't been any mistakes."

After my conversation with Galeazzi and subsequent conversation with Cushing, I received a letter from Mother Pasqualina, asking why I was staying in Boston. Clearly, Cushing had convinced her he preferred for me to stay in Rome. Further, she thought Sennott and I had worked my transfer out in the chancery office and Cushing had simply signed off on a done deal. When Pasqualina learned of my conversation with Cushing, she decided to ferret out his true intention about where I should work. Although Mother Pasqualina wanted me to return to the North American College, her primary concern was that I obey the orders of my bishop. She wrote to Cardinal Spellman to find out what he knew. Cushing had contacted him some time ago to learn whether he objected to moving me to Boston. Once Mother Pasqualina learned Cushing's will, she gave up urging me to return to Rome.

Cushing got into this mess because he was afraid of offending anyone important. His inability to take a position and stick to it, despite the consequences, would get him into lots of hot water. Down the road a piece, he repeated a similar performance during the Second Vatican Council, to the absolute horror of the conservatives in Rome. A hotly-debated subject in Vatican II centered on whether the bishops shared authority with the pope in decision-making. Cushing had agreed to defend the conservative position which favored supremacy of papal authority, apart from any consultation with bishops. The established bureaucrats in Rome prepared a speech for Cushing to deliver to the bishops assembled at the Council. At the Pope John Seminary, I received the coded telegram advising the Cardinal it was time to arrive and deliver the speech. In Rome however, the liberal camp cornered him before the session. He agreed to deliver their statement in favor of collegiality, the principle of shared authority between pope and bishops. At the session of the Council, Cushing flabbergasted the Roman crowd with a speech favoring collegiality. In a conference that evening to graduate students, he announced collegiality as the way of the future and the only course which made sense in modern times. It is ironic that although at the Council he advocated for bishops to share authority with the Pope, neither he nor the American bishops thought to share authority with either the clergy or the laity.

Back in Boston, I took up my new duties as vice chancellor. Interminable requests for dispensations came by mail and by phone. Most required no thought. The system itself set the rules and the fees for dispensations from such practices as church announcement of a forthcoming marriage. Dispensations really piled up the fees, which went to the senior rule enforcer, the Apostolic Delegate in Washington, D.C., the Pope's official agent in the United States.

The typical clergy approach to canon law contributed to chancery office busywork. Most clergy behaved like business school graduates, unable to allow exceptions absent a case study authorizing such exceptions. As seminarians, the clergy had regurgitated memorized theses and rules. Consequently, they lacked the capacity to think critically and evaluate risks. To be viable, an option had to appear in a list of allowable moves.

In lieu of risk-taking, the chancery offered opportunities for domination over clergy and lay people. For my part, I turned routine paperwork over to the secretaries, instructing them to confer with me only before denying a request. I failed to perceive any relationship between my present duties and the grand ideas for which I left the Navy. I felt I was marking time and accomplished little except organizational efficiency, for which I earned a reputation as the black knight of rule enforcement. Far removed from the bridge on the ship of state in Rome, I saw myself as a branch manager of rules. I felt boxed in. Life began to make less and less sense.

One of my worst experiences came from Bishop MacKenzie. He ran the marriage tribunal and one day, out of the blue, he invited me to witness the forbidding of a marriage. Into the courtroom we went. He climbed up to the high judge's bench, and a nervous young woman sat below him. She had petitioned for permission to marry a second time. He growled at her like a pitbull straining at the leash and denied the request. Further, he warned her, avoid any notion of a civil marriage. We left as abruptly as we entered. I thought the performance shocking. Even with my dedication to rules, I marveled that the woman had put up with his performance. MacKenzie, on the other hand, thought he had performed his duty admirably. I felt ashamed. I wrote to the Cardinal and asked for another assignment, with a carbon copy to Bob Sennott. He asked me to reconsider, but I wanted out. Two days later, the phone rang.

"His Eminence would like to see you." I walked across the lawn to the Cardinal's residence and into his study.

"I have been wondering how long you would last over there," the Cardinal said. "Have a seat. How about the new national seminary for delayed vocations?" asked the Cardinal.

He had undertaken this new venture after the bishops of the United States had turned it down, fearful it could not work. The Congregation of Seminaries in Rome had asked the American bishops to start a separate national facility for older men who wanted to enter a seminary. Cushing saw this proposed facility as an opportunity to recruit men from the business and professional worlds. Traditionally, men in the United States started seminary training immediately after graduating from high school or college. Where his brother bishops had seen only problems adapting rigid training and community living to mature and independently-fixed personalities, Cushing saw the possibility for a nationwide fund-raiser and a new source of manpower. He had spent four years on the preliminaries. I saw it as an attractive opportunity and said so.

"Fine. Don't say a word about this until I send you a letter of appointment. Meanwhile, consult with Ed Murray. Tell him I am going to make you the rector of the new seminary for delayed vocations."

Monsignor Ed Murray puzzled many observers. Ostensibly well-versed in theology, a probing exchange with him usually exposed a superficial grasp of the field. Typical of his generation, his theology was derived from memorized theses. Psychologically, he evidenced more than average insecurity. His erect bearing and large frame helped cover it up. Although he could speak clearly and distinctly when required, he mumbled softly in conversation. He lived on a make-believe stage, modulating his voice to manipulate his audience. Seminarians tagged him as "Mumbles."

To Cardinal O'Connell, Cushing's predecessor, Murray had appeared to be a bright and promising graduate of the North American College. O'Connell had made him the relatively young rector of St. John's Seminary, which belonged to the Archdiocese of Boston. He displayed blatant favoritism. Student rooms across the corridor from his quarters at the end of one wing became known as Boys' Town. There, the favored students lived, ostensibly because of their functions as house officers. As one of the seminary's four masters of ceremonies, I lived in one of these rooms during my first year of theology. While I appreciated the recognition, I disliked the segregation. I also thought it evidenced colossal bad judgment.

By the time Cushing decided to put me in charge of the new seminary, he had fired Murray from St. John's Seminary, the facility of the Archdiocese of Boston. Neither one ever told me why. Assigned as pastor of Sacred Heart Parish in Roslindale, one of the largest, he made occasional stopovers there. He traveled at the drop of a hat. In Rome, he stayed at the best hotels. His access to cash flow amazed me. His life's purpose appeared to be as an ecclesiastical gossip. Ed kept daily count of the number of days from his dismissal as rector of the seminary. Invariably, at every meeting he gave the tally. Accustomed to receiving a new four-door Ford every year at the seminary, he held on to his last one. It presented a pathetic spectacle as it acquired dents and irreparable damage. Worn out by rust, beyond all repair, it eventually died. His star set with it.

I telephoned Ed Murray with Cushing's message. "I'll be right over to Chancery," he replied. "We can talk in my car." He arrived, and I went out to talk with him. "I have a letter appointing me the Rector," mumbled the ashen-faced Murray, slumped down over the wheel, his dream world smashed. I felt embarrassed. Many years ago, he had singled me out for study in Rome, and the result came to this. I learned later he had negotiated in Rome with the Congregation of Seminaries as Cushing's agent for details of this proposed seminary. Now, out of the blue, I wiped him out.

Once again, Cushing stuck me in the middle, thanks to his habit of ducking the role of bad guy. Like his dismissal from the diocesan seminary, Murray could not get over this blow either. I never consulted him about the seminary nor did he visit. Yet, one day he told me he hoped I didn't mind that he told the Cardinal I relied on him for advice. Feeling sorry for him, I merely shrugged my shoulders. A few years later, when purple kingdom keepers challenged the theology taught at this new seminary, he championed the conservatives' cause. He even took prospective candidates to lunch in an effort to convince them to not enroll. According to Cardinal Cushing, Murray went to the Congregation of Seminaries in Rome to complain about the Pope John Seminary, a complaint that eventually led to my resignation as rector.

His relationship with Cushing never became clear. Murray told me Cushing never once invited him to sit down, despite countless visits to Cushing's office. Cushing told me he submitted Murray's name three times for promotion to bishop. "The last time, I even had his buddy John Wright prepare the paperwork," Cushing protested. Murray's value to the Cardinal ultimately came when Murray served as a convenient and willing conduit to authorities in Rome, testifying to the Cardinal's old-school theology and loyalty to the system, while Cushing simultaneously encouraged us at the seminary to blaze new trails. Cushing remained consistently dedicated to working opposite directions on the same street.

A letter of appointment as rector gave me a new schedule for 1963. Show up every day at Cushing's desk at 4:00 PM. At our first meeting he gave me his one directive. "You do whatever you have to do to make the place work. I'll do the only thing I know how to do, raise money. We're in this together."

Raise money he did. He kept a small pocket-size diary in which he recorded his daily take. Occasionally, he produced it to show me his monthly totals. His target in 1963 was one million dollars a month. He met it regularly and exceeded it frequently. This cash he collected personally, apart from all other institutional and parish sources. His predecessor had enjoyed a swimming pool in the basement of the residence. Cushing floored it over for a mimeograph and mail room. He went anywhere he could get a check and keep his name and activities in the public press. His goings-on made standard fare for Monday morning newspapers, usually front page. His latest picture, project, or wisecrack filled conversational voids in board rooms, bridge parties, and parish halls across the city. His was the only dining room table I ever ate at with the telephone sitting on it, albeit red to match his new hat. Probably no other cardinal in the world published his telephone number, answered it himself when all the help had left, and told unwelcome callers that they spoke with the janitor.

Clearly, not one dime of his income went to his own or his relatives' bank accounts. His family took out a mortgage on their house to get money for the trip to Rome when he got the red hat. Embarrassed, he allowed three of his sisters and a brother to be included in his official party. One sister, too ill to travel, died while the family watched the ceremonies. I arranged for a private family dinner at the Hotel Roma, a novelty for them, who were grateful to have him show up on Thanksgiving Day. His sisters went home for the funeral services while his brother stayed in Rome.

The new seminary, named Pope John XXIII National Seminary, received national publicity. Two sets of letters went out, one to every bishop in the country and the other to each of the 63,000 priests on parish assignments. We invited unmarried or widower applicants 30 years of age or older, set the length of the course at four years, said we would consider life experience in lieu of a college degree, and announced we would open in September 1964. Both letters appealed for funds, to be sent directly to the Cardinal. Cushing became pen pals with contributors from all over the United States, particularly military chaplains who took up collections designated for the seminary.

The first few men accepted to the seminary created great publicity. Cushing capitalized on the human interest value in their stories. Pope John Seminary sat on his front burner. My daily reports provided grist for his mill and items for his weekly column in the *Boston Pilot*, the newspaper of the Archdiocese. The new seminary became my ticket for admission to the inner sanctum of the purple kingdom.

—10—

The Inner Sanctum Plots Sabotage

Vatican Council II started its formal sessions in 1962, when I was still working in the Chancery. Designated as a consultant to the Council's Commission on the Discipline of the Clergy and Christian People, my attitudes in that capacity mirrored loyalty and obedience to the system. At the time I planned the seminary, although I envisioned new approaches to training, I still stood firmly behind the line of authority extending from the Pope through the bishops.

The construction and furnishings of the new facility kept me busy. Student and faculty recruitment and program design filled my days and nights. The assignment of these multiple tasks to a single individual demonstrated the scope of the rules. Church authorities considered operation of a seminary to be so ordered that matters almost took care of themselves. Fortunately, I received valued advice and council from a group of five volunteers, all young seminary professors in Boston.

Vatican II was establishing a climate of debate and inquiry, hitherto unheard of in Roman Catholic circles. This new-found freedom first expressed itself through experimental changes in the liturgy. Changing the liturgy meant changing the position of some the furnishings of the sanctuary, notably the altar. The architect wanted a decision on placement of the main altar. I thought it should be in the traditional alignment, against the wall. The group of consulting professors, closely following developments emerging from Vatican II, wanted the altar turned around so the celebrant could face the congregation. This seemingly innocuous variation from tradition carried with it grave implications.

Neither Cushing nor I then perceived the implications. In retrospect, both of us acted arbitrarily when we rejected the professors' request out of hand. In and of itself, changing the altar's position would not have violated any dogma of faith, but it would have allowed some exercise of a new ceremonial freedom at the expense of tradition. My professor consultants, all personal friends, quit in frustration.

In defending their position, the five consulting professors criticized the Cardinal and me as being uninformed and hence incapable of making proper judgments. Automatic obedience was no longer a given. To be obeyed, orders must be rational. The Cardinal and I could not see any validity to their position; we thought they were merely unhappy because they could not call the shots. Our assessment went as far off base as the reading of a situation could get. Typical of the myopia and ignorance in the purple kingdom, we stuck blindly by the old rules and the old way of doing business; we could not see that profound and healthy changes were in the air.

One year later, Cushing sent me to the Congregation of Seminaries in Rome, the agency charged with seminary surveillance worldwide. The Cardinal wanted to be certain that our plans met with approval in Rome. There, I discovered my experience with these professors involved far more than a local power struggle. Headquarters in Rome had watched as theologians published a growing avalanche of credible and new perspectives. One functionary summed up his assessment with the opinion that the more advanced of these radicals formerly would have shown the courtesy of joining the Protestants. Of all the challenges the theologians were making to traditional rules, none equaled the sensitivity of challenges to authority.

Archbishop Staffa, the Chief Executive Officer of the Congregation of Seminaries, told me to expect exactly the type of rebellion demonstrated by the five consulting professors who had wished to turn the altar around and then quit in frustration at my intransigence. He told me this attack on obedience had taken root around the world. We continued to discuss the extent of the insurgency and plans to regain control.

In Rome, Archbishop Staffa asserted, they realized the freedom of the Council could not be banned. Indeed, the Congregation itself must act with utmost prudence vis-a-vis the Council. But careful plans, quietly made, already spelled out how to regain control of authority after the Council closed. The infection of radical ideas would be treated in due course. For now, the Congregation could only watch and identify the trouble makers. When the Council ended, they would clean them out. Further, the Consistorial Congregation, the agency which passed on all promotions to bishop, now screened out all nominees except those of demonstrated loyalty and obedience to Rome. If by chance one of these reformers got promoted to bishop, I should know it would be unintended.

I went along with these sentiments, convinced of the need to maintain authority. I encountered no one in the hierarchy who even suggested an evaluation of the merits in the new ideas. Blinders to any new thinking went with every job slot. The rules, not the Gospel, ran the show, although we failed to grasp the significance of this fact.

The Congregation of Seminaries advised me to dismiss at once any professor who espoused radical ideas. I did not agree with this directive as I thought academic debate essential to understanding the great themes. If new ideas challenged basic principles, the voice of authority could always step in, as it did when Cushing and I unilaterally decided to preserve traditional placement of the altar. However, I kept my thoughts about academic debate to myself. Clearly, Pope John had set off a revolution within the ranks.

Rebelling against the subversive power in rules requires brave souls to operate outside the rules in the hope that enough people will follow and create new rules more in tune with goals. The five professors in Boston worked at the beginning of such a local process. They asked critical questions about liturgical practices, dug into their origins, and analyzed the theology behind them. They came up with new ideas and new rules to bring practices closer to original purpose. This type of liturgical innovation was relatively safe stuff in contrast to changes which threatened the scope of authority in the hierarchy. It took several years before Vatican II's challenge to authority was fully manifested. For now, at this initial stage, I determined to make intellectual honesty the operative norm for the Pope John Seminary, expecting the basic structure of authority to remain intact. I thought a bridge could be built between the old and the new ideas. Without being aware of the consequences, I had embarked on a duel to the death of one or the other. I never suspected the power of domination inherent in the old rules, despite the extremity of the situation after Vatican II, when vested interests collaborated to defy the decrees passed by a General Council of bishops and endorsed by the Pope.

The seminary organization and the new building began to come together. Cushing wanted a simple, practical organizational structure. Incorporation papers established me as president and treasurer. The Cardinal appeared on the letterhead as founder. A Board of Trustees, appointed from pastors in Boston, functioned exclusively to interview prospective seminarians. Cushing made all the critical policy decisions. He insisted that I make the screening decisions. Above all, he wanted the seminary to have popular appeal, which he measured by the inflow of cash donations.

In the summer of 1964, before we opened the doors, Cushing and I became apprehensive about policy differences between us and Rome. For one thing, a cloud hung over our heads about the length of studies. We had advertised four years, although we knew the Congregation of Seminaries favored a six-year schedule. Were there other issues lurking out there that might cause conflict with the Vatican authorities? In retrospect, I think the Cardinal also wanted to know whether Ed Murray's disappointment in not being appointed rector had caused political problems in Rome. I set off for Rome and unexpectedly ended up at the Pope's desk.

—11—

Gale Force Winds of Rule Change

I entered a big room with frescoed walls. A small, gilded desk stood off-center, with one chair on each side. Pope Paul VI took one of them, and I sat down on the other. Without question, I respected his position as the head of the church, but I also saw him as the end product of a successful election campaign. The realism in my present thinking contrasted sharply with the awe I had experienced during World War II at being in the presence of Pius XII. Then, as I had stood with thousands of cheering GIs in the crowded basilica of St. Peter's, I had wondered how he and God communicated. Now, I thought of John XXIII's observation upon being elected Pope: ". . . the end of the road, but the top of the heap."

I had requested this audience because Archbishop Staffa, chief operating officer of the Congregation of Seminaries, had told me that Paul VI had reacted enthusiastically to my reports since he himself had started a training program for older men during his tour as Archbishop of Milano. Knowing of the Pope's interest, I filed an application for an audience, expected to stand in a long line of visitors and exchange a few words with the Pope as he passed along. With luck, I could get a picture with him which would be very useful for fund-raising.

Meanwhile, I contacted Count Galeazzi. We fixed a date to visit a mountain estate he had just bought, having sold the seaside one where I had recovered from pneumonia. The weather turned awful, wet and raw. We came back a day early.

The concierge at the Hotel Roma handed me an envelope from the *Maestro di Camera,* the official in charge of audiences with the Pope. In no particular rush to open it, I tossed it on the desk in my room, fiddled with the furniture arrangements, and sat down to attack the mail. I slit open the envelope from the *Maestro di Camera* and could not believe what I read. I shook my head and read it again. Sure enough, a private audience with the Pope that very day, one hour hence. It could easily take one hour to cross Rome's traffic to Vatican City and another half-hour to navigate to the papal quarters. I saw big trouble in the making. Why had I gone for overkill and asked to see the Pope?

Although tempted to scrub the audience with a telephone call to the *Maestro di Camera,* I decided to go for it, gambling that attendants would shuffle the order of audiences. The first challenge came from the cassock with its mile-long string of buttons. Off came the black one and on went another black one with red piping. I grabbed the long purple cape, flew out the hotel door, hailed a cab and headed for St. Peter's Square. I had intended to bring all sorts of propaganda material to show the Pope first-hand. It all got left behind.

The taxi driver easily found St. Peter's Square but threw up his hands when he reached Vatican City. I knew the streets and alleys of this neighborhood and directed him to the courtyard where the elevator connected with the papal apartments. The elevator operator spotted me leaving the taxi, rushed out into the street, threw both arms into the air and wanted explanations for why I had dropped out of the sky after a sudden and long absence. I convinced him to talk later. "Get the elevator going," I said frantically, "I am running late for a meeting with the Pope." From then on came greetings and questions from all the people along the route, making me feel like I was playing that old child's game of going through the hot oven.

Convinced I would find out what happens when you are late for the Pope, I ran to the antechamber to the Pope's private reception room. There, Mario Stoppa, the layperson in charge of the flow of visitors, greeted me. He calmed me down. Paul VI was still talking with his first appointment. Thank God for the ecumenical movement. Cardinal Bea, in charge of all ecumenical activity, continued to sit at the Pope's desk. I now explained to all the Pope's men why I had disappeared so suddenly two years ago and what I was doing now in Boston.

One of the monsignors on duty, Loris Capovilla, had served as personal secretary to the late John XXIII. I had first met him during the conclave which elected Pope John. We spent the time now reminiscing and roaming from room to room. At one point Capovilla opened a tapestry-covered door and with a sweeping gesture waved me in. I thought he suggested a look at some unusual treasure in another room. As I wheeled around the doorpost, in front of me, taller than expected, stood a smiling Pope Paul VI, saying how pleased he was to see me.

We did a Gaston and Fauntleroy act about who sat down first. He did. My training aboard the *Philadelphia* stood by me. I sat at ease in front of the Pope and saw myself as part of a problem-solving process. He explained how he took older workers in Milano and housed them in one wing of the regular diocesan seminary. There, they studied until ready for the philosophy and theology courses with the regular seminarians. The Pope was excited about opening a new source of manpower when traditional sources were declining. Hearing the progress of a seminary in Boston exclusively for this purpose, he became enthusiastic about its prospects. Anxious to share the experiences of the operation in Milano, he offered to arrange for hospitality at the seminary and insured that I would have access to whatever I wanted to learn about that program.

After I had thanked him for his interest, I said that Cardinal Cushing wished to invite Archbishop Staffa for the dedication ceremonies. The Pope readily agreed and volunteered to write a personal message for Staffa to bring with him. He also offered to pray personally for the seminary's success. He opened the drawer of his desk and fished around for an appropriate souvenir. He came up with a four-inch circular silver medallion in a red box. It had an image of himself on one side and the papal keys on the other.

We parted warmly. Delighted to have gotten along so well with the top man and to have a hand in a project he thought so important, I saw nothing of the storm ahead. Both of us would be hunkered down in opposing bunkers, stuck with opposite views of organizational authority.

I reported the content of the audience to Staffa. Word spread of the Pope's enthusiasm, and the seminary enjoyed enviable status in the purple kingdom. Staffa, one of the most reactionary of bureaucrats, admitted nobody knew how to run a seminary of this type. He added that I should carry out whatever plans I thought best. He would prepare a list of items to consider that were not to be seen as directives, but as items for review when designing seminary policies.

I could hardly believe my ears. He had said precisely what I needed and wanted to hear, setting me free from the traditional rules for seminary operations. Cushing and I had already determined to make the seminary an adult operation. When Staffa gave me the green light for independent decision-making, I was delighted.

Shortly after the conversation with Staffa, I took the overnight sleeper train to Milano. At meals and in meeting rooms, the seminary faculty reflected the aura of backstairs connection to the Pope. Conversations took place in hushed tones, with serious facial expressions and sudden silences when outsiders came within earshot. I met the person in charge of the "worker" program which held special classes for men in one wing. They did the equivalent of two years of college and then went into a six-year seminary routine with traditional seminarians. Seeing no relevance of their program to ours, I got through the formalities and returned to Rome and Boston. Before leaving, I asked Galeazzi to arrange an oil painting of John XXIII for the seminary. I asked Pasqualina to arrange a set of gold-embroidered vestments for solemn ceremonies. The painting came through as a gift from Paul VI. The vestments came with the bill, as expected.

Staffa and the faculty in Milano talked about "workers" who would be trained for the priesthood. Even Paul VI used the term. It took me a while to grasp the implication. In their minds, candidates came from the manual labor class, not the professional or business segments of society. They restricted adult admissions to those with less than a fifth grade education. Exclusion of the educated convinced me then of the low esteem in which they subconsciously held their profession. Now I see another example of entrapment by the rules. Business and professional men presented a threat to the status quo. Accustomed to making independent decisions, they would be less compliant with artificial rules than uneducated adults. Professional skills and organizational know-how would threaten superiors who knew only church rules. Apart from the whole issue of delayed vocations, all American seminarians have suffered from the stifling training intended for fifth graders, as Staffa's subsequent letter made clear.

True to his word, Staffa sent a 2-page outline of suggestions and ideas. In general, he proposed relaxation of traditional seminary discipline. Encourage adult seminarians to mix with the local community, to meet with people, to visit families in their homes, to maintain social contact. Do not supervise and regiment them as if they were younger seminarians. In short, treat them as adults. The concluding paragraph defined what the Archbishop meant by adult vocations. It meant anyone 18 years of age or over. These guidelines should have been in place already in seminaries across the United States. Staffa demonstrated how little he knew about the age and education level of men admitted to seminaries in the USA.

Traditional seminary rules originated in Italy, where seminarians began their training at about the age of 11, when they reached fifth grade. The American bishops, ignorant of this age orientation and conditioned to obey without question any and all rules from Rome, condemned generations of American seminarians of college age to a training program designed for Italian grammar school boys. It is a tragedy that tens of thousands of dedicated individuals in the United States have submitted themselves to this malformation, believing it necessary for them to live as children under continuing supervision before they are qualified to preach the Gospel. Blind obedience to rules based on a foreign culture defined the operations of seminaries in the United States. Any question of meaning or purpose of the training went along for the ride. Subversion of purpose by the rules flourished.

Staffa's letter helped explain the agony with which most clergy made decisions. It helped explain also the paradox of overinterest in rules of canon law on the part of graduate students from the United States, despite their cultural conditioning to independence. Instead of developing free and responsible decision-makers, the seminary system turned men into boys worried about the rules of their housemasters.

If the role of the priest confined itself to liturgical functions, there might be justification for such programming. However, once one considers the importance of preaching the Gospel to help people make sense out of life, these rules subvert the purpose of the church. They turned out clergy who knew only rules based on the Italian culture, and who had more difficulty than was necessary in dealing with thier personal lives, and the family, marital, and social difficulties of their parishioners.

The Pope John seminary began classes in September 1964. For the first few months, students followed a prescribed routine which evolved into self-directed routines decided upon by the students and the faculty. Study ranked as the primary discipline. Twin principles of collegiality and the rule of conscience minimized rule-making by the administration. We set up forums for decision-making. Student and faculty forums did ongoing analyses to make life easier and the atmosphere more conducive to learning. Faculty status had to come from the content of their lectures since students had more years and life experience than any of their mentors.

Our behavior ran counter to standard seminary operating procedure, where the rector ran a one-man show and made all the rules. I saw students and faculty as resources to be tapped, rather than liabilities to be managed. The student forum organized itself like a New England Town Meeting. Delegates from the forum met regularly with the faculty and administration to review operations, hammer out improvements, air grievances and make decisions for collective corrective actions. Faculty, too, met as a body for shared decision-making. It worked. One faculty member's lectures frequently could be read in the textbook. After a student and faculty meeting, the lecture content thereafter expanded on the textbook. Students owned automobiles and parked them on campus, with no restrictions on their use. Designated parking areas were enforced. Unknowingly and thanks to the dynamics of the forum, the seminary went ahead of the Naval Academy; there, only the senior class enjoyed automobiles on campus. Student automobiles on campus dramatized the enormous difference in style between Pope John Seminary and all other seminaries in the Catholic system where use of automobiles by fifth graders was unthinkable.

The rule of conscience, under the general norm of concern for needs of others, made detailed rules unnecessary. We published only such items as mealtimes and class schedules. Rules of behavior, developed by consensus in student and faculty forums, reflected the Gospel and set the standards for individual conduct. We tried to distinguish authentic needs from personal desires. Needs of others came before personal convenience. The silence necessary for study could not be impaired by one person's fondness for loud music. Everyone contributed to the effectiveness of the program. Students maintained the facility in a high state of cleanliness and good order. Each student spent at least one hour per day at institutional housekeeping chores. Many also worked at fund-raising and library upkeep. I thought these chores were necessary to help instill habits of personal practical service for the needs of others. To provide students with complete housekeeping services would have aggravated attitudes of privilege from clergy status, the antithesis of the notion of Servant Church emerging from Vatican II. Over time, a community of mutual support in post-Vatican II style began to emerge at the seminary.

By the time the second year rolled around, Vatican II had concluded. Faculty no longer speculated about its outcomes. Most of the faculty had come from recent graduate studies in Rome. There, they had discussed the issues with the experts at the Council and listened to its debates. To teach the decrees of the Council became the order of the day at the seminary.

The winds of rule change now blew at gale force, to the utter dismay of the purple kingdom. You could eat meat on Friday. Latin disappeared from the liturgy. Penance and fasting lost value both as punishment-reduction vehicles and as salvation devices. Limbo as the destination for the unbaptized disappeared. A new order started to emerge. Useless obedience to unproductive rules became channeled to the fundamental task of responding to the needs of neighbor.

Most American bishops failed to understand this dynamic. To them, rule changes denied the legacy of the past and broke with the deposit of faith left by Jesus to the apostles. Convinced they had acquired adequate theological knowledge in the seminary, they suffered a trained incapacity to understand and explain Vatican II to the laity. Perplexed laity lost out, left to drift and understand as best they could the startling developments of this Council in Rome. Confusion reigned. Few faculties in the world taught the theology emerging from Vatican II, which meant few new clergy were being adequately trained. The dedicated and instructed layperson faced a monumental dilemma. How could a past practice that one had invested so much energy and sacrifice in suddenly be decreed worthless? The Pope John seminarians and faculty lived in the thick of these discussions with our neighbors. Our chapel services held standing-room-only crowds.

Theologians assumed a new status. From their ranks came the intellectual support for the changes. The granddaddy change of all turned the pyramid of authority on its head. If the Holy Spirit is diffused throughout the People of God, then the people are the seat of authority, with the Pope and bishops as their servants. As I had heard from the bureaucrats in Rome, such an approach caused real panic in the upper echelons of the purple kingdom. In fact, debates after Vatican II circled around the purple kingdom's efforts to preserve the pyramid of authority, with the Pope at the top.

Scripture studies produced profound changes, with radically new understandings. Adam and Eve became understood as a story rather than as an historical event. The story gave writers of Scripture a picturesque way to describe the contentious condition in which humans found themselves. Canon lawyers joined the band wagon. They removed unreasonable rigidity in procedures. Divorce and remarriage became possible. The impulse for change gathered momentum throughout the world.

During these dynamic times, legitimate authorities in both the secular and religious worlds were subject to critical evaluation. Old obediences determined to have outlived their usefulness lost legitimacy. Old values got new forms of expression. New ways of thinking about ethics zeroed in on whether the practice promoted or hindered human welfare. Useless rules sloughed off from the human condition.

Seminaries around the world stood in steady and severe decline. Most of them divided into two warring camps, roughly according to new and old faculty. The Pope John XXIII seminary thrived at full capacity with vigorous theological debate. Our student base spread to Australia and Canada. Money poured in. One day Cardinal Cushing arrived with Cardinal Garrone, who recently had been appointed head of the Congregation of Seminaries by Pope Paul VI. After 20 years of experience as the bishop of a diocese in France, Garrone's approach to administration contrasted sharply with that of most career bureaucrats, as evidenced by his world tour for a hands-on inspection of seminaries.

Garrone and I toured the facility. He conversed at length with students and faculty. The size of our library holdings astonished him. An extensive collection of recent theological works in English complemented a complete collection of writings by the Greek and Latin Fathers of the early Church. The enthusiastic and mature approach of our students, their obvious dedication to the mission of the Church in modern times, and their grasp of theological concepts impressed him profoundly. He made no bones about telling Cushing his unbounded admiration for what he saw and heard. He acknowledged it as the one bright spot on his trip. Garrone's stamp of approval temporarily spiked the guns of the purple kingdom system-keepers, although they continued to grumble against our radical teachings. By mail, by conversation, constantly, we invited bishops to join in a dialogue and to come and visit the facility, yet most refused the invitation.

The time was approaching when I would soon have to choose sides. I found myself with a job offer I could refuse.

—12—

I Cross the Rubicon

One night in the early spring of 1968, the phone rang in my room, and I heard Count Galeazzi on the other end. He was in Washington, D.C. for the annual meeting of the American bishops, and he went directly to the point of his call. Bishop Martin O'Connor had just resigned. Would I agree to submission of my name for appointment as rector of the North American College?

Instantly, I saw the move as a stepping-stone to a very senior spot in the hierarchy. Overall, I still stood in good shape within the system. Cushing had told me the time neared for him to promote me to bishop. Friends in Rome, like Galeazzi, continued to have stature, regardless of the reigning pontiff. The new seminary stood out as a bright spot in an otherwise dismal landscape. Such factors easily overcame sideswipes from reactionary nitpickers in the purple kingdom.

I also knew the reality of the North American College. My role would be to sustain the purple kingdom of rule-keepers. The freedom I now enjoyed would vanish. Already the duel shaped up between new ideas based on decrees of Vatican Council II and those of the old school contained in the *Baltimore Catechism*. This battle repeated the David and Goliath match-up because the bishops held entrenched and established power.

By this time, I had spent three years at Pope John Seminary. During meals I listened to the faculty debate points of theology. Like many others in the Roman Catholic world, the faculty worked to understand and develop the implications in the documents of Vatican Council II. As professional theologians, they developed bridges between old and new ideas. They did this in collaboration with our adult students, not the usual run of seminarians fresh out of high school or college. Each one came with demonstrated success in a career path. Each gave up this success to help others make sense out of life, exactly the perspective theologians hoped for from the renewed orientation of the Roman Catholic Church.

Mealtimes with a table of experts became my private three-year seminar in theology. By now I thought we had developed concepts and structures to bridge the old and new ideas. At the same time, I thought most bishops could not conceive of such a process. At the time, I thought them just plain stubborn, intellectually lazy, or both. Today I hold them harmless as victims of the pathology in every organization which causes rules to displace goals and subvert them. The changes of Vatican Council II could be judged by them only as threat to turf and perks.

Bishops believed the salvation of the human race required them to maintain position power. Turf and perks thus came ahead of the mandate to preach the Gospel. This organizational disease ran from the Pope and Roman Curia on down through the ranks of bishops, monsignors, pastors, and their assistants. Decrees of Vatican II called for unwanted and painful surgery. Rule-keepers in the purple kingdom naturally sought to avoid such treatment for their disease.

Although I was an administrator, I now considered the authoritarian approach improper for the Church's mission to preach the Gospel. Absolute rule by one man in a parish, a diocese, a seminary, or the entire Church, sounded as out-of-date as use of a bow and arrow in World War II. The level of public education and complexity of variables in people's lives clearly made autocratic decision-making unreasonable. Besides, one-man rule opened the way to whim as rule.

The theological orientation of the purple kingdom reflected the Middle Ages. Rule-keepers assumed that life in the era of the atomic bomb and Sputnik was no more complex than life in a medieval farm town. However, clergy no longer ranked with the privileged few who could read and write. Domination by princes and the divine right of kings went long ago into history books. Yet the purple kingdom still kowtowed to princes of the church and proclaimed divine right of bishops.

The proper use of authority by religious leadership seemed to me to be motivational, to develop consensus around principles and to encourage their application. I thought it arrogant for a church leader to proclaim any specific as the will of God. Only those involved had the ability to weigh the circumstances. Were I still in the Navy training a gun crew, this would have been too loose a process. Admittedly, in certain situations, discussion, debate, and reflection become counter-productive. Nobody expects fire fighters to arrive at the scene and hold a forum to get consensus on the proper window to use for the fire hose.

While I see the role of religious leadership as motivational, pragmatically the leaders also have to manage the organization. Thus, the management component opens the window for the creation of rules which end up overtaking organizational purpose. It is natural for leaders to focus on management issues. After all, organizational improvements can be seen and charted for improved efficiency and effectiveness. Heads and money can be counted; wealth can be assessed. On the other hand, religious leadership at the normative level can be measured only indirectly, through the deeds people perform in service to their neighbors. True leadership at this level comes only from the example of service to others. It calls for unrelentingly hard work to give a consistent and inspiring example. An easier and natural path is to manage the rules.

Dedication to rules made it seem to many that organized religion had outlived its purpose. Concern for neighbor had become institutionalized. The population was taxed, and a portion of that tariff paid for human services. Social workers served the needy. Legal advice replaced clerical advice. Political action could augment human services, while church leaders were largely seen as fossils squabbling over rules. People were already voting with their feet. Church attendance had declined steadily and seminaries around the world watched the downslide in enrollment numbers. Unanswered was the dilemma of where Catholics could find leaders for their spiritual needs.

My many contacts with American bishops demonstrated that their primary interest concerned obedience to themselves and conformity with established rules. They saw no conflict between rules and the Gospel. Many bishops considered the church as a kind of fishnet woven with rules. The faithful, caught in this network, could be delivered to salvation. From a different perspective, I saw the Church as a resource to promote the freedom of the Gospel in a milieu of self-directing and self-responsible individuals. A clear and simple directive had guided the apostles: preach by example.

Only the Dutch hierarchy, of all the national organizations of bishops within the Church, endorsed and published a catechism to explain the decrees of Vatican II. This effort stood as a tribute to the perceptiveness of these bishops. The purple kingdom condemned their work, thereby offering a sad indication of the theological wasteland in the ranks of the rest of the world's bishops, who thereby also testified to their enslavement by the old rules.

Galeazzi's call put me at a decision-making crossroads. Would I take the comfortable road, hoping eventually to become a cardinal, or would I continue along the uncertain path for beneficial change? Convinced I could not live a charade by fronting for those addicted to the *Baltimore Catechism,* I told Galeazzi that the timing was premature. The Pope John Seminary, still at a tender stage, ought not risk a new hand at the helm. Perhaps I could be considered for the next round at the College.

Galeazzi was completely silent on the other end of the line. Finally, he murmured a weak OK. We both hung up. I had dead-ended on the fast track. Some years later, he wrote to say numerous reports and news clippings came to him about my activities. He neither liked nor understood the happenings in the Church. However, he was convinced my behavior must stem from good and valid reasons, and, regardless of the outcome, I always would have his trust and confidence.

At the time of his call, I disliked very much turning him down. But, after my education at Pope John Seminary and my awakening to this new way of life, I could not live in the job of defending the purple kingdom; it made no sense. Galeazzi's phone call galvanized my thoughts. Henceforth, I would work to publicize the reforms of Vatican II. We turned to the public press, knowing it would offer the best hope of getting the message out. Newspapers were glad to cover our story because change and conflict in the staid old Roman Catholic Church sold papers. Bishops avoided the secular press. We at Pope John Seminary stepped into the void.

Birth control and its morality now held center stage, a hot topic for debate. We taught there could be no such thing as a universal prohibition, a position which gained ever wider acceptance in Roman Catholic circles worldwide. On the other hand, Pope Paul VI thought any form of artificial birth control was an intrinsic evil. He soon declared so, unilaterally, in the encyclical *Humanae Vitae*, a papal directive to the church worldwide. By making this declaration, Paul VI not only violated a Council decree he recently had promulgated in which he declared popes shared decision-making with bishops, but he also signaled his intent to restore the pyramid structure of authority and create a showdown between old and new rules. The purple kingdom made adherence to Paul VI's declaration against birth control the litmus test for orthodoxy.

—13—

Eye of the Storm

The Pope John Seminary was gaining ever-wider audiences. Our faculty blazed the trail coming out of Vatican II. Papers delivered to professional societies of theology and canon law spread the ferment of new ideas. Some of our students balked at the changes from the catechism they learned. All of them struggled with new forms of expression and the loss of comfortable customs. But they were able to understand and accept the changes in theological approach, with consequent changes in rules, because knowledgeable faculty explained the rationale.

Purple kingdom dwellers lacked both the will to study new ideas and the professional help. They felt they had learned all the infallible facts of religion when they were in seminary. They really stepped up to the plate of life with two strikes against them. They lacked contact with up-to-date faculty, and they thought their theology was fixed for eternity. I spoke with several bishops who complained about writers without having read one word of their works.

Our publicity reached even to the *Today Show*, which did a segment on the seminary. We made news for two reasons: full-capacity enrollment of unique students and grasp of Vatican II. Positive national and international publicity, together with statements of support from around the Roman Catholic world, firmed up my belief that we sailed on the right tack. Perceived as a breath of fresh air in an otherwise stale atmosphere, money poured in to the seminary.

By May of 1968, the first graduating class of 24 priests went on duty in 19 dioceses of the United States and two dioceses in Australia. Pope Paul VI wrote to Cardinal Cushing, sending his congratulations. "From a heart filled with paternal joy, do We send greetings to you, beloved Son and to the twenty-three ordinands to the Holy Priesthood who form the graduating class of that pioneering institution, the Pope John XXIII National Seminary. We give thanks to Almighty God that the work of the seminary has been so richly blessed and that the candidates have proved themselves worthy of the highest confidence and trust, as also for the numbers and quality of those applying for admission."

That same summer, the second class of 22 men, ordained to the diaconate, went as interns to 20 dioceses in the States to preach and experience parish duties. As a general rule, pastors complained about the products of seminaries. However, our graduates and deacons received universal praise. They bridged the old ideas and the new. Our graduates knew more than rote memory of rules. They could explain the theological reasoning behind the new teachings. Written evaluations from pastors especially praised the interns' preaching. They conveyed a message in language people understood and which made sense in contemporary society. With these letters in hand, we could document the high quality of our product.

It came as no surprise, in July of 1968, to hear George Collins from the *Boston Globe* on the phone. He asked for comment on a new papal encyclical coming in over the wires. Frustrated in his attempts to locate anyone to comment, he had called the editor of the *Boston Pilot,* Monsignor Frank Lally, who told him to call the Pope John Seminary.

Collins knew that the Encyclical *Humanae Vitae* basically condemned all artificial means of birth control. Such a strong stance made good copy, and the *Globe* wanted a statement. Faculty at Pope John wanted to use the chance to comment as a way to let our far-flung students know where we stood on the document, since at the seminary we taught a very different position on birth control. As the text was coming off the wire, Collins invited us to come in and read the encyclical and make our comment.

Four of us headed for the *Globe*, read the complete encyclical and released our statement. We thought the Pope was wrong, and we said so. What Pope Paul VI had just pronounced about birth control could not be sustained scripturally, theologically, or historically.

Sitting in the barber's chair the next day, I learned a more tactical approach.

"Why did you say those nasty things about the Pope?" the barber asked.

"Lots of people think the Pope is God speaking," I replied vigorously. "We want them to know there are other opinions."

"No, no, when the Pope speaks, you cheer, 'Viva il Papa'," the barber advised. "If you don't like what he says, just don't pay any attention to it."

This barber, raised to adult life in Italy, probably produced the sanest of all the reactions.

The fury of the North Atlantic during a mid-winter storm seemed mild in comparison to reaction in the purple kingdom. Ocean storms pick no designated targets and they eventually subside, but kingdom dwellers decided to fight us to the bitter end. The rule changes we had already advocated gave them indigestion, but denying the Pope's dictatorial power stirred up all the adrenaline in the kingdom, which closed ranks. A campaign started to recall students and shut down the seminary. Several factors made it difficult for them to close the seminary.

Our alumni base spread across the country. Our graduates turned in impressive performances at the parish level, even in the judgment of conservative bishops. We enjoyed wide-based public support in lay and clergy sectors. We stood out as a new bright light in the supply line of vocations to the priesthood. Above all, we collected most of our operating funds directly from clergy and laity, with little help from bishops.

Prior to our public statement, I had given Cardinal Cushing maneuvering room and sent word of our intention to bomb the encyclical. I gave him the option to keep silent or to tell me to hold off. If our action proved successful, he could claim he authorized it. If, on the other hand, it became a disaster, he could claim innocence. Hearing no response by the late afternoon, I assumed he favored sending up a trial balloon.

Our statement was one of a multitude condemning the encyclical. Many theologians around the world issued similar statements. In the United States, more than 800 faculty members at Roman Catholic institutions of higher education endorsed a document in opposition to the encyclical. Mail poured in about our comment. Cushing didn't talk to me directly about our comment, but he sent me letters he had received condemning our action. He never once sent a favorable letter. I knew he received them because people mailed me copies. As the storm brewed, I waited for him to make the first move.

His problems mounted. Monsignor George Casey called me. He had grown up in South Boston with Cushing and had gone through St. John's Seminary with him. He put affluent St. Bridget's parish in Lexington, Massachusetts on the map as a progressive center of ecumenism and Vatican II theology. Rather than build a parish school, he had established a Christian education center. Author of "Driftwood," a column in the secular press, he kept abreast of the times, knew the score, and understood Cardinal Cushing as few others did.

"I just finished speaking with the Cardinal," Casey told me. "I told Cush to stand by you. If he takes any action against the seminary, I will not give him another dime. Instead, it will all go to you."

One evening the phone rang. Cushing himself spoke. "You gave that institution the kiss of death. You are all done." I thought his real upset was that our comment had thrown a monkey wrench into his money machine.

"Lots of people agree with us," I replied. "The mail is running six-to-one in our favor."

"All you did was take the popular stand," he retorted. "You did not stand by the Church. I don't know what is going to happen now but you have had it."

He hung up abruptly. My years of pulling rabbits out of the hat for him no longer counted. Somebody had worked him over, and I stood condemned without a hearing. I figured his perspective would return once the smoke cleared. I wrote and asked for an appointment. He granted it by return mail.

Rather than use my key to the front door of the Cardinal's house, I rang the door bell. I wanted to be ushered in. Shown to the formal conference room near the front door, I waited alone at the long table. I felt like a stranger in the house where I used to sleep on the second floor when Cushing went out of town. He did not want the nuns on the top floor to be alone in the building. Now I sat where I used to see others waiting as I had waltzed upstairs, taking for granted my access to his study on the second floor.

In he came, not in his shirt sleeves, but in vest and Prince Albert coat, with a long and solemn face. He shut the door and sat at the head of the table. The closed door went with the full dress as chilly signals of a change in our relationship. I was no longer the trusted ally with whom he had sat in his shirt sleeves, pulling a little black book from his back pocket to share the secret daily tallies of his cash collections.

He showed no interest in our reasons for opposing the encyclical. He merely stated that if I didn't back off from our public stand, he would close the seminary. His reasoning ran the gamut from an insistence that the professors were making a damn fool of me to the stern voice of authority laying down the law. I explained that the issue really concerned freedom of conscience.

"What's conscience? Who knows? You want to be loyal to this conscience," he said. "I am loyal to authority. I take orders. I do what my superiors tell me. I am standing by the Church. If you and the other professors out there refuse to accept this doctrine, we will close the seminary. It is impossible to find qualified professors to replace them. We will then assign all of you to parishes."

"Your Eminence," I said. "There is something I have to say. The issue is not birth control; it is the role of conscience. Millions of people got stuffed in ovens because individual consciences were ignored. If we can't teach that an informed conscience is superior to any law, then you won't assign any of us to parishes. We will all walk out of the priesthood."

He sat stunned. Such dimensions had never entered his head. In an abrupt change of tone and demeanor, he replied, "You do what you have to do and I will do what I have to do. I am loyal to those guys. I am not mad at you. Remember this, we are still friends."

We shook hands and I departed. Asked by his secretary how the meeting went, "He's adamant," snorted the Cardinal.

As I learned later, the Apostolic Delegate, the Pope's link with bishops, had told Cushing to remove me, but Cushing's political instincts, rather than blind fear of authority, prevailed. As he explained later, he thought that removing me and closing the seminary would cause a major riot.

Students returning from summer vacations reported that their bishops first intended to withdraw them from Pope John Seminary. The performance of the two classes on duty in parishes caused them to change their minds. Not only did the full complement of students return, but four additional dioceses sent students. The reactionary element, meanwhile, spread the rumor that bishops had not sent students back.

One night, Cardinal Cushing called the seminary three times looking for me, gave up, and left a message. "Bring in the books. A special committee will set procedures for closing the seminary." When I got the message, I called the Cardinal's secretary, Joe Maguire, a rock of stability in an otherwise unpredictable house. I asked for Cushing to meet with the faculty before he sat with the special committee. I argued that closing the seminary for the wrong reasons would be tragic. I didn't want the Cardinal to say six months from now "Why didn't somebody tell me?" I gambled on Cushing's sensitivity to his place in history and the argument was effective: Cushing agreed to meet with the faculty.

At that meeting, Cushing brought Monsignor Al Julien, a canon lawyer from the old school, truly dedicated to all the tenets of the purple kingdom. Again the Cardinal showed no interest in theology. Political consequences of my removal occupied his mind. He asked point blank what the faculty would do.

"All of them would walk out," they replied.

"I'll tell you what else would happen in Boston. I'd have 300 priests out picketing," added the Cardinal. "What kind of a budget are you operating on?" he asked.

"We have an annual operating deficit of $125,000," I answered.

When he heard this, he lost all interest in moving the books to the chancery office. I raised that amount annually.

After discussing the books, we asked to be present when he sat with the special committee the next day. We didn't want to make an argument or present our case, but only assure that any data presented correspond to the facts. The Cardinal said that no action would be taken against the seminary, but agreed that the rector should attend the meeting along with one member of the faculty.

The meeting the next day was stormy. When the purple kingdom defenders saw me and the faculty member in the very room they had entered to organize the dismantling, they registered astonishment. Some became very angry. At group meetings, I had noted that Cushing invariably addressed the person to his immediate right. I had therefore asked Dick McBrien, the faculty delegate, to sit in that spot before the group arrived.

McBrien made a logical choice as faculty delegate. First of all, the Cardinal held him in high regard. He had authored a letter Cushing published on the Servant Church, for which the Cardinal had received copious favorable publicity. His reputation as a theologian already had reached national stature; his weekly column syndicated in the Catholic press explained the developments emanating from Vatican II.

The Cardinal began by asking Dick to summarize yesterday's meeting with the Pope John faculty. He did, with Cushing adding his own comments to the narrative. When the group heard that the Cardinal had reached the determination to take no action against anyone at the seminary, it went into shock. Bishop Tom Riley, a former rector of St. John's Seminary, a man noted for law and order and with a reputation for scholarly purists, called the procedure highly irregular. Nobody had invited him to yesterday's meeting nor had he received a copy of any minutes.

Bishop Riley then rose from his chair. With solemn, measured speech, he proclaimed it his duty to declare the Archdiocese in schism, which meant the existence of a group cut off from loyalty to the Pope.

He looked at Cushing for a reaction. None came. The Cardinal sat there like a sphinx. Becoming very agitated, Riley gathered more and more steam as he described what he thought about theology as taught at Pope John Seminary. Then, he sank down into his chair and looked at Dick McBrien for a reply.

McBrien's analytical skills, fueled by his substantive knowledge of theology, presented such a tightly-reasoned response that Bishop Riley reacted only with stuttering reaffirmations of his opening statement. He became so jittery, I expected to witness a heart attack. Dead silence settled in. Clearly, McBrien had caught Riley unable to swim in waters over his head. A philosopher by training, his lack of depth in theology stood revealed to the Cardinal, as well as his loss of cool. Cushing broke the silence.

He singled out Ed Murray by name and asked whether he wished to say anything. Ed ducked any debate about theology by asking McBrien who should sit in judgment of physicians. Cushing then asked each of the other attendees to speak their minds. They offered little. The Cardinal got down to business.

"Prior to this meeting," he said, "the Apostolic Delegate and I discussed the situation at the Pope John Seminary. The Delegate authorized me to settle the matter." What Cushing did not tell the group was that the Delegate had also instructed him to remove me.

Turning to McBrien, Cushing asked, "Dick, suppose one of the members of the faculty were removed. What would be the reaction of the others?"

"We all would walk out," McBrien replied without hesitation.

Cushing then asked Broderick, the rector of the Boston seminary, if there would be any difficulties at the Boston seminary if action were taken against Pope John's.

"We would have trouble at St. John's Seminary were any steps taken against the Pope John Seminary or its faculty," Broderick answered.

Cushing asked in vain for an assessment of the clergy's reaction and then gave his opinion.

"Well, let me tell you what would happen with the priests of the Archdiocese," Cushing said. "We would have at least 300 of them out on the sidewalks, and God only knows what would happen in colleges around the city. I do not know where the rest of you spend your time, but I move throughout the Archdiocese and talk to everybody. I am telling you the city is not taking the heads off this crowd. They have great support."

I cheered silently. At last, reality hit the fan.

"If you want me to blow up the Archdiocese of Boston, you can have my job," continued the Cardinal. "It is something I will never do. My policy has always been not to act when in doubt. Right now I have many doubts. There is an old saying which goes, when in doubt . . ."

Ed Murray piped up and said, "Punt."

"That's right, punt," said the Cardinal, and he continued, "There will be no action taken against anybody at that seminary and that is the judgment I have been empowered to make by the Apostolic Delegate."

Tom Finnegan, the chancellor of the archdiocese, asked whether Cushing should make some prohibitions against the faculty speaking out. Cushing put him in his place.

"These are responsible people. They will continue to teach, preach, and write. That is the end of it."

Outside the Cardinal's residence, standing on the front steps, Ed Murray started to harangue us as we headed for our cars. He obviously disliked the unexpected turn of events. I told him he should have spoken his mind during the meeting with Cushing. He hadn't spoken out then, but, as I soon found out, he would go over the Cardinal's head and voice his complaints loud and clear.

Purple kingdom devotees never give up. They are subject to a double whammy from the rules. Secular bureaucrats judge their rules as sacred and become afflicted with devotion to their defense. In the purple kingdom, the added affliction is to crusade for the rules because they come from God. Cushing called me soon after the meeting.

"You are in trouble. Listen to this."

He read from a letter written by Cardinal Garrone, head of the Congregation for Christian Studies, the new title given his old job as head of the Congregation of Seminaries. He heard of trouble at the Pope John Seminary. The rector was saying strange things. What could Garrone do to restore peace to this institution which promised to be of such great service to the Church?

"Obviously, Your Eminence, somebody has been talking to him," I said. "The best resolution would be for me to fly to Rome, sit down at Garrone's desk and discuss whatever concerns he has, face-to-face."

"Good idea," Cushing said. "I'll tell him you are coming. Go over there and make peace. He is a friend of yours and thinks highly of you. Don't be a crusader. Agree to whatever he wants you to do."

Before I left for Rome, Cushing told me the only person he knew who visited that Congregation recently was Ed Murray. I did not tell the Cardinal that I knew Murray would have lacked credibility in Rome absent an endorsement from the Cardinal. Cushing was playing his same old tricks: playing Murray off against me and trying to keep both of us on his side, while keeping himself out of trouble.

—14—

Victory in Rome

Off to Rome I went, bringing two faculty members with me: John Mahoney and Jack Finnegan. Prior to leaving, I posted on the bulletin board Garrone's letter to Cushing and invited students to comment by letter directly to him in Rome. Many did, thereby demonstrating our unusual seminary practice of taking students into seminary affairs. The letter campaign and the inclusion of the faculty showed Garrone I did not play alone behind closed doors. I also hoped to discredit Ed Murray as a witness in light of his past attempts to dissuade students from enrolling.

On the eve of my departure, Murray called to tell me he had met at length with Garrone in Rome and that their conversation had centered on the difficulties at Pope John Seminary. He offered to brief me on the concerns of the Cardinal. I thanked him but said whatever bothered Garrone would be explained by him when I got to Rome.

It was fortunate that Cushing was willing to write to Garrone and tell him that I would come over to discuss the issues with him. Without the letter, Garrone could have refused to see me and continued to deal with Cushing directly, leaving me out in the cold. Cushing's letter reduced a faceless bureaucracy to a person. Whatever sat on the table became an issue between Garrone and me. Garrone was an extremely powerful ecclesiastic, regarded as the only cardinal in the Roman Curia able to make policy decisions without prior clearance from the Pope. I was counting on Garrone's personal visit to the Pope John Seminary and his assessment of it as the brightest spot in the whole system as my ace in the hole. Finally, I knew that I had friends in Rome, and that my reputation there was still good.

As I walked in for the first meeting, I was met by an old acquaintance, Monsignor Marchisano. At first I thought I had found an unexpected friend at court. However, his greeting, formal, starchy and strictly correct, signaled trouble ahead. I wondered why he seemed embarrassed. Then it hit me; he had acted as Murray's mole, feeding the rumors into headquarters. I remembered being surprised that he had visited the United States when we had dedicated the seminary. During that visit, he had stayed at Murray's rectory. Now I knew trouble lay ahead.

Marchisano brought me directly to Garrone's reception room. He appeared immediately and sent for his number one assistant, a German archbishop. Both behaved cordially. After preliminary pleasantries, I took them through a loose-leaf notebook of material. We reviewed technical data about the seminary, including financial information, as well as copies of my speeches, together with their reports in the secular and religious press. Copies of letters from cardinals, archbishops, bishops, and pastors singing the praises of our graduates and summer interns made my basic case. We agreed to meet the next day at 10:00 a.m.

At the next meeting, Garrone said he would hesitate to send students to the seminary, were he the bishop of a diocese. He did not like what I had said about celibacy. His observation told me two things. First, he had not read the speeches, because I made no reference to celibacy in any of them. Secondly, I played in a game with the deck stacked against me. Garrone did say the letters from the pastors impressed him highly, but asked whether I had included every letter. Fortunately, the packet contained 46 letters from the 46 pastors with whom interns worked.

The seminary unquestionably ranked as an excellent work, Garrone said. However, it did need to be kept in perspective. I seemed to say delayed vocations solved all the problems of the Church. Marchisano chimed in with a speech about the importance of this seminary. Perhaps I did not realize the extreme need for discretion, given my position. More than the rector of an ordinary seminary, I guided a new institution that was getting international attention.

The German archbishop, short and on the plump side, tried to get the conversation down to business. With considerable stammering and rolling of his eyes, he said voices had come to their ears declaring celibacy to be an infantile practice. I admitted that I had written those sentiments in a letter to an editor of a magazine called *Ave Maria* when he had asked for comments on an essay called "Celibacy, the Faded Challenge." The Cardinal expressed displeasure at my commenting on celibacy without reference to a document which Paul VI published. I did not tell the Cardinal I saw no merit in the Pope's remarks.

The meeting broke up on reasonably friendly terms, with no mention of big problems. All we had talked about was a letter to the editor of a very small magazine. I knew there had to be more in store. I met up with Mahoney and Finnegan who had spent the day going all over town and getting the scoop from their acquaintances. The two faculty members told me local gossip had it that I had come to Rome to get sacked.

The next day's meeting dealt with the press. Marchisano said they had a pile of clippings over a foot high with statements I'd made. I responded that I was glad that people were interested in religion, and it was important to respond to their concerns with accurate information. Sensing an opportunity, Marchisano moved in for the kill.

"It is our understanding the Pope John Seminary is conducting a campaign to overthrow the papacy."

The absurdity of the statement, plus the seriousness with which they believed it, struck me as funny. Obviously, they were the ones who had been set up, not me. They had been getting bad information and had fallen for it, hook, line, and sinker.

"How can you say such a thing?" I asked.

"You publish those sheets that are sent around the country attacking the Pope," Marchisano replied.

"What sheets?" I asked.

Garrone, with a scowl on his face, which I suspected he intended for Marchisano for getting him into this pickle, told him to get the sheets from the file. We sat in silence until he returned. Marchisano produced a couple of pages, badly reproduced, of material I recognized immediately as the syndicated column written by Dick McBrien, one of our faculty. The poor quality of the reproductions told me they had been reproduced dozens of times, creating a long chain of transmissions which had finally ended at this office. We printed the originals at the seminary on an offset press, using seminary letterhead. We mailed them primarily to Roman Catholic military chaplains to help them keep up with developments in theology. Several hundred others also used this service. I told them the purpose and audience of the sheets and offered to send them a complete set when I returned to the seminary.

Dead and awkward silence set in. Obviously, they had played a bad hand. They probably felt they'd been misled by selected and disjointed bits of information. Marchisano broke the spell. He suggested we remove the names of the seminary and the Cardinal, as well as my own, from future reproductions. Otherwise, it looked as though the content carried official Church endorsement. I listened politely, without comment. The monsignor dredged up more.

"You and your professors attacked the Pope on television."

"Monsignor, we never appeared on television to attack the Pope."

"How could that be?"

"I don't know, but we never spoke against the Pope on television."

"Well, there is the question of your statement about the encyclical on birth control."

"Monsignor," I protested, "800 professors have signed a similar statement. If we are in trouble, so are they. If we are to be dismissed, so must they."

The Cardinal interjected with one word.

"Silence."

His command swept the question off the table. At the time, I did not know of the instructions for bishops to deal locally with all problems relating to the encyclical, without recourse to Rome. Since the encyclical was a forbidden topic in Rome, the Cardinal changed the subject. He declared it perfectly clear that the seminary was excellent in every respect. As a matter of fact, it stood as a model institution. But somehow, an atmosphere of distrust had been generated. The problem was to find the cause of this distrust.

I thought the Cardinal was about to zero in on me. Although the work itself passed muster, one man was acting in a way that would discredit the institution. I waited for the boom to fall, but no one pressed the point. In the vacuum, I decided to speak bluntly, hoping to ward off an attack.

"Your Eminence," I said, "this atmosphere of mistrust is the work of conservative bishops and their supporters. They can't understand our position on the encyclical or our support for Vatican II."

Again, dead silence. Then the German archbishop came in like the tuba, sputtering the same old refrain.

"Yes, but there was what you had to say about celibacy."

Garrone ignored him.

"What do your professors think about this situation?" asked the Cardinal.

"Two of them are here. You can ask them tomorrow," I said.

"Perhaps they might greet the Cardinal in the corridor after the meeting," suggested Marchisano, ever the true system keeper averse to direct talks with the troops. After a moment's silence, Garrone suggested that a letter from him endorsing the seminary might help. I suspected that Garrone was looking for a graceful way out of the controversy.

"What do I do now?" I asked Marchisano as he escorted me to the elevator.

"I think you should write a nice letter to the Cardinal," he advised. "Say you are sorry you said some of the things you did. You see them now in a different light and are certain there will be no complications in the future."

I thanked him for his counsel. I was sure that he would go back to Garrone and report that I had seen the light and would appear tomorrow with a letter seeking the forgiveness and blessing of the Congregation for Christian Education.

That night, the two professors and I got little sleep. Instead, we wrote a two-page document that restated our positions in the clearest possible terms, with supporting arguments. We made a dozen photostat copies in the morning, and the three of us headed for the Congregation. The two professors took the group by surprise, as did the efficiency of copies for everyone.

As the Cardinal read the document, he got more and more agitated. His hands shook. He became uncharacteristically nervous. I thought his position worse than mine. His letter to Cushing indicating that there was a problem at the Pope John Seminary had opened a can of worms. He knew we had an enviable track record with our graduates, and furthermore, we were accustomed to working with the media, an area out of his ken and feared by the ecclesiastical bureaucracy. If we went public with the politics of the attempt to suppress the seminary, we could cause great embarrassment.

Garrone put the paper down and addressed the professors, trying to establish a more friendly level of conversation.

"How do you like Rome? It is fortunate you came here so that we can help you."

John Mahoney spoke up.

"Your Eminence, all over the city they tell us our rector is here to be murdered. Who has spread rumors about us? Are they bishops? This is a terrible way to expect seminary professors to live and work, knowing voices and rumor are what influence such an important place as this Congregation. I would like to know who says what against us and our rector."

The Cardinal replied that no bishop had complained to him about the seminary. He offered to produce the file and told an astonished Marchisano to get it. Mahoney interrupted.

"Never mind, Your Eminence. It's better we do not know. If you say there are no bishops, we will take your word for it."

The German archbishop jumped in.

"You know the things your rector has been saying. Can you stand behind them?"

Both professors said they could. They knew of only one nonprofessional statement, the one in *Ave Maria* magazine.

"You will teach the encyclical, will you?" asked the Cardinal.

"Of course," I responded. "Before Roman Catholics make moral decisions, they must consider official Church teaching."

This time the dead silence became embarrassing. I had defined our outlook on papal authority, and they did not contest it. Had such a declaration of freedom of thought been made to any purple kingdom type in the United States, there would have been wringing of hands, gnashing of teeth, and angry denunciations to the Apostolic Delegate.

Cardinal Garrone concluded the meeting by offering to write a letter endorsing the seminary and its rector, which we could publish in the press. I was jubilant. Such a letter would implicitly declare that we had won out over the rumor mill. Procedurally, Garrone continued, he would send a summary of his findings to Cardinal Cushing and ask if Cushing had other concerns. If not, Garrone would send the letter of endorsement for publication.

I volunteered to remain in Rome until Cushing responded. Garrone insisted that such a stay was unnecessary. Nothing stood in the way of the letter for publication, unless I knew of problems which the meetings had not addressed. I did not.

John Mahoney, a professor of theology, summarized the situation as we rode the elevator down from the Cardinal's office. With all the weighty theological questions we could have analyzed, the most frequent topic had been celibacy and the strongest issue had been birth control. Said Mahoney, "The trouble with this crowd is not theology, but biology."

—15—

Scuttled by the Rules

When Cushing received Garrone's letter, he immediately drove out to the seminary, bringing the letter with him. Garrone had not only endorsed the rector and the seminary, but he declared the rector exonerated, the seminary exemplary, and the case closed. But this letter was not for publication in the press; Garrone intended to send a second letter for this purpose, once assured that Cushing faced no other concerns about the seminary.

Financial largesse always indicated the state of Cushing's mind. At my initial visit to report back from Rome, I had asked him for a one-million-dollar endowment fund. When he came to the seminary with the letter, he offered to give us three million and saw no difficulty raising it. He agreed also to a proper board of trustees. We wanted the seminary less subject to pressures on him from the rulekeepers.

Cushing made copies of Garrone's letter, but I have no idea what he did with them. Shortly after Garrone's letter arrived, Ed Murray showed up for his second visit to the seminary. I guessed trouble lay ahead but could not imagine the specifics. With the air of an apostolic inquisitor from the Middle Ages, he asked what response he should give to Garrone's letter. He implied that he'd received a commission from Cushing to draft a reply. Before he did so, he wanted to know my plans for the future of the seminary. I thought he displayed colossal nerve. I had already sent a reply to Garrone at Cushing's direction. I thought Murray fished for information and told him my future plans were none of his business. He left in a huff.

Garrone's second letter of endorsement, intended for use in the press, did not arrive. I began to regret I had left Rome without it. Finally, a second letter arrived, addressed not to Cushing but to me. It contained a new list of conditions, two of which were particularly onerous: a guarantee against speaking out and the appointment of a new board of trustees, all of whom were to be drawn from an attached list, all of them reactionary bishops. I tossed the letter in the wastebasket. Garrone had gone back on his word, which, until then, I considered good.

Strange remarks by Cushing began to surface. He made statements which were completely inaccurate, saying that our enrollment had declined, and furthermore, that we were asking him for money which he could not afford. In fact, our enrollment was at full capacity, and we were raising more money than our annual budget required. It became clear that some new force worked against us, although we did not know who exactly had the Cardinal's ear or what that person's leverage was.

While rumors of these remarks came floating back to the seminary, when Cushing was speaking to the faculty he volunteered that as long as he remained the Archbishop, the rector would not be removed and the seminary would not be closed. He next told me privately that he knew of only two people who had gone to Rome to talk to Garrone about the letter: Ed Murray and John Wright, by now a cardinal in Pittsburgh. Obviously, Murray and Wright had to have had Cushing's endorsement to visit Garrone. Cushing had consistently worked both sides of the street, telling me what he thought I wanted to hear, while simultaneously supporting Murray's efforts to overthrow me.

Conservative bishops soon made the second letter moot. Their new tactic hit pay dirt. They announced that alumni from the Pope John seminary would not be accepted in their dioceses as long as I remained the rector, regardless of what Rome said. Dedication to old rules so dominated these bishops that they could ignore the findings of their senior officer in Rome. Garrone in Rome had endorsed conscience as the ulti-

mate norm; they held obedience to authority as the ultimate
norm. The rules held them by their throats.

For me to crusade on behalf of Vatican II made sense, but
not at the expense of the seminary or the students. I went to
Cushing and offered to resign from the seminary. "You are
making me a very happy man," he responded. "If you hadn't
resigned, I would have had to close the seminary." He concluded
our meeting by saying, "You must know you are politically
dead, but don't worry. I will take good care of you."

At a subsequent conference with the faculty, he introduced
the new rector, Monsignor Mulcahy, whom the Cardinal had
advised to not interfere with the faculty. He also explained his
predicament. The Apostolic Delegate and a crowd of conservative bishops had pressured him continually to remove me from
the seminary. Convinced such a step would bring political disaster, he'd decided that he would plead poverty and shut down
the seminary, ostensibly because of budget problems.

Unlike tenured faculty, I either carried out corporate policy or gave up management responsibility. Cushing suggested I
pick any parish I wanted, debt free, a generous departure from
his normal procedure of imposing a debt for a new pastor to
liquidate. But a parish assignment held no attraction for me,
and instead I suggested graduate business school. I wanted to
learn why anyone would cooperate with any organization. At
the University of Massachusetts in Amherst, I enrolled in the
three-year doctoral program of the Business School. At age 48,
I became a student again and lived in a college dormitory. The
Cardinal paid all my bills, and sent me $100 each month for
pocket money.

At the Business School, I lucked out once again with my
mentors. The Dean, Jack Conlin, suggested I take a new
faculty member, Joe Litterer, as my advisor. He had just been
recruited from the University of Illinois. I did, and any visions
of an easy stroll in the park went out the window. Instead of
philosophy of business, my patch of academia became organizational behavior. Joe Litterer set the agenda, and I studied the
relationship between self-interest and bureaucratic behavior. I
learned that the players in the purple kingdom had acted in a
very predictable way. Down through the centuries, they had
obeyed the dynamics inherent in all bureaucratic organizations,

while they and the faithful usually thought they'd been complying with divine guidance. Instead, self-interest had triggered the behavior of many popes and bishops who'd felt that delivering the Gospel was dependent on their status of authority. In fact, ecclesiastical turf and perks became more important than the Gospel message, because the hierarchs made rules which supported their empires at the expense of the Gospel. One need only look at issues such as the history of slavery, the discrimination against women, and the old laws exempting clerics from the jurisdiction of civil courts to see evidence of this pathology.

Standard organizational pathology explains the institution's loss of integrity. The rules necessary to structure an organization eventually subvert the purpose of that organization and ultimately become synonymous with the organization. When Cushing had said I did not stand by the Church, what he meant was that I did not stand by the rules,

Nor is this analysis mere speculation. Church authorities in Rome at the time of the Vatican Council told me of their repulsion for the new reforms and described plans to clean out the reformers after the Council. Further, they insisted that none but those with demonstrated loyalty to old rules from Rome would be promoted to bishop. I was told to dismiss from the faculty anyone who promoted the new ideas. The opposition of authorities in Rome to Vatican II can be understood when one realizes that Vatican II threw out the status and authority accumulated over centuries.

My three years of study started to wind down. Before taking any action with respect to my next assignment, I met with Medeiros, the new Archbishop of Boston. In a cordial exchange, he made it clear. No place existed for me within the Archdiocese of Boston. Initially, I thought his statement outrageous. Canon law obligated him to a two-way contract; he was obligated to provide my maintenance, and I was obligated to work for the Archdiocese of Boston. Quickly I realized that his statement was an invitation to resign from the priesthood.

"Why don't we both be very honest?" I said. "I should resign from the priesthood." Obviously relieved, he rose at once from his chair.

"Let's walk over to the chancery office," he said. Medeiros directed the immediate preparation of papers for my resignation. I helped with the details. A few weeks later I received the document from Rome granting me status as a layperson. I was officially liberated.

Starting a new life as a layperson was challenging. Past my fiftieth birthday, and with a long career behind me, I had to begin over again. Help came from a surprising quarter, in the form of a lively, accomplished woman whom I'd first known many years previously when she was a soda clerk at Donovan and Fallon's, a drug store a block from St. Mary's Church in Charlestown. The assistant pastors gathered there on Saturday nights after confessions. Behind the counter worked Helen Chin, a bright, vivacious clerk in a white smock. In between customers, she carried on an easy banter with the clergy. Not a parishioner, she lived a few doors down the street where her family ran a laundry.

Nearly two decades later, I found myself at the Pope John Seminary and needed to work through degree procedures with the Commonwealth of Massachusetts. I called the Board of Higher Education. Instead of the Chancellor, a woman's voice came on the line.

"Hi. This is Helen Chin. Remember me?"

Right away I recalled the friendly clerk behind the ice cream counter. I guessed she held some clerical position, had overheard my name, and picked up the phone to say hello.

"Helen Chin. The last time I saw you, you were stuffing ice cream cones in Donovan and Fallon's."

"Glad you remembered," she said. "What can we do for you?"

"I need to find out how the seminary can grant degrees."

"I can help you. I am assistant to the Chancellor."

Pleased to have discovered a friend at court, as well as with my memory recall, we discussed the procedures. Polite, but brief, chit-chat ended the phone call. She asked whether I ever came to downtown Boston. If so, how about lunch. I accepted, but the lunch would have to wait. I had business to complete in Rome.

Back from my sessions with Cardinal Garrone, I cleared up minor details of our application. I then asked about that lunch. We settled on a date. Her suggestion bowled me over. "How about the Ritz?" Startled, I first thought to suggest less expensive surroundings. Lunch at the Ritz Carlton made a quantum leap from ice cream at Donovan and Fallon's, but I decided she must know what she offered and agreed.

We met in the lobby. Instead of the white smock of the ice cream clerk, she dressed in keeping with the quiet elegance of the Ritz. Vivacious as ever, she led the way up the wide carpeted marble stairs to the dining room. The maitre d' greeted her like returning royalty. He showed us to a corner table, overlooking the Boston Public Gardens. I might have pulled off such a performance in Rome, but had no such clout in Boston. I was impressed.

Bishop O'Connor would have relished the setting. Fresh-cut flowers decorated every table in the vast room. Tables sparkled with crystal goblets, sterling silver, and fine porcelain on wrinkle-free linen. Multiple service persons in spotless, freshly-pressed uniforms attended each table. Helen had captured the one table with the prime view. She delivered an unavoidable message. She had actually come a long, long way from the ice cream counter at Donovan and Fallon's.

Several years later, after my resignation from the priesthood, and a wholehearted but failed attempt to refinance Belknap College in New Hampshire, I turned to Helen Chin's network. Through a friend, she introduced me to John Larkin Thompson, President of Blue Shield. He circulated my resumé. Phil Gillette, Thompson's executive vice president, hired me. By this time, relations with Helen evolved from that of an old-time acquaintance, to a helpful resource person, and a voice of reason in turbulent times.

She still lived at home with her mother in Charlestown and had earned a master's degree in education from Boston University. She had gravitated toward politics and public service, interests she had acquired early on listening to the politicians who congregated in her father's laundry. In between visits to Boston's Chinatown, she translated encounters with emergency rooms, doctors, and nurses. She also translated understanding between the two communities, Chinatown and the wider one in which it sat. She began paid public service during summer vacations as a state house clerk. After graduation, she began full-time employment in the House Speaker's Office, whence she has continued to move on through increasing levels of responsibility in the executive branch of Government.

When we decided to get married, we knew we had to cut potential criticism off at the pass. Helen had invested a lifetime in State service as a public manager and hoped to continue. I expected to work in the Boston area. A resolution had to be found. The Chancery Office stood as the epitome of orthodoxy. It issued the rules and enforced them. Anything the Chancery said got obeyed. Helen and I were pronounced man and wife there. Our wedding announcements notified the world that the ceremony took place in the chapel of the Chancery Office of the Archdiocese of Boston. More legitimizing a setting could not be found.

I became a staff person at Blue Shield of Massachusetts. When Phil Gillette, the executive vice president, took me to lunch to celebrate my 60th birthday, he told me a story. Shortly after I began work at Blue Shield, Dick Wright, a physician and brother of Cardinal John Wright, went to Gillette's office. He asked for my dismissal because I had behaved so badly against the Church. Gillette cut Wright short, saying he had hired me for my ideas, not my theology.

Gillette possessed unusual talents for a bureaucrat. His job description required him to manage internal operations. He could be as irascible and unpredictable as Cushing, a factor which kept me at a distance. Like Cushing, he displayed street smarts. He could step aside from operations, assess the external environment, and gauge the gap between performance and corporate mission. I came on the scene when Gillette started plans for new ways to finance health care.

He interviewed me at length and assigned me to a planning group which designed blueprints for action by the operating divisions. I found myself in the perfect organizational spot to correct deviation from corporate goals. Our planning group enjoyed the authority to enter any operating area, collect data, develop plans for corrective action, and make a critique. Such dynamics matched the need for agents of change to operate outside the organizational plan.

We came up with many blueprints, some of which called for significant changes in operating rules. To implement the more radical of these changes took more courage than the corporation could muster at the time. Maybe the old nemesis of fear to change sacred rules stalked the offices of the ultimate decision-makers. Then too, we may have been too far ahead of the times, as Cushing once had told me. With the benefit of hindsight, I can report that one of these blueprints became operational as a major competitor of the corporation, Bay State HMO.

After retirement from Blue Shield, I visited the Naval Academy in Annapolis. There, many strands came together.

—16—

The U.S. Naval Academy Shows the Way

"This place sure has changed," I said to myself, watching the earnest faces of midshipmen striding back and forth for classes. Fifty years after my student days here, I sat on a green wooden bench near Tecumseh, a replica of the figurehead of the ancient *U.S.S. Delaware*. From the bench, I could see the vast expanse of yellow brick in front of the facade of Bancroft Hall, the dormitory building. Its wide granite steps and curving ramps created a permanent grand stage for football rallies. We had marched in formation up those ramps en route to meals in the mess hall. We had also lined up in uniform on those yellow bricks to march silently to academic buildings. Today, midshipmen criss-cross the same bricks wearing diverse uniforms. Instead of slide rules, they carry pocket calculators and blue tote bags with computers. In contrast to our silent marches, today's independently-proceeding midshipmen converse amicably in subdued tones. Nobody loiters. The atmosphere exudes quiet energy and a sense of dedicated purpose.

A question haunted me. Why did the Naval Academy thrive so vibrantly with intense competition for enrollment in its 4500-member brigade, while seminaries of the Roman Catholic Church shriveled like discarded produce, many of their buildings sold for other purposes? Both functioned to train future leaders for service to others. Why did service in the Church sink to such a low level of esteem? Why was the fate of the Academy so different?

As I sat on the bench, I became aware of the quiet. At first, the silence was eerie. Then, it dawned on me. There was no drummer on the knoll in front of the chapel. He used to beat out the cadence as we marched to class in lock-step ranks. But midshipmen in this generation march to an inner directive, free to develop their own talents and interests. At the Naval Academy, self-direction has replaced programmed monolithic behavior. Today, the curriculum is loaded with options.

"They don't march to class any more," complain some of the alumni who are also shocked by the sight of women wearing midshipmen's uniforms and living in Bancroft Hall. In our day, women walked the corridors of Bancroft Hall one day a year as escorted guests of graduating seniors. Notable now is the conspicuous presence of blacks in the brigade. Contrast this with the tale we heard in 1939 of a black student who overcame all obstacles and survived until the final exams, only to be thrown out. The score of his lowest subject got scaled as a failing grade. All midshipmen with that score or below went out with him. It blows all the fuses in old timers' circuitry to think of black women giving orders from the bridge of a warship at sea. "Women here are a passing fad," say some of the old alumni.

Obviously, the Academy scuttled many of its time-honored rules. Driven by its well-defined mission to prepare future leaders for the Navy, the administration took the attitude of Admiral Farragut at Mobile Bay. "Damn the torpedoes. Full speed ahead." Let the chips fall where they may. When it became clear the system needed an overhaul, the rules got evaluated under a single decision principle: Would a change help or hinder the Academy's mission in today's society?

Alumni alone as administrators could not have reached the psychological capacity to radically alter the rules. Management literature makes it clear that members of all organizations become infected with a pathology that exalts standard operating procedures. The literature also indicates the disease to be incurable, unless an outside force intervenes. The Academy fortunately possessed such a force in its Board of Visitors. Prominent citizens, educators from prestigious universities, and captains of industry took a hard look at Academy rules and made recommendations for sweeping changes. It is a tribute to the sense of selfless purpose on the part of the Academy's leadership that they were able to listen to these recommendations. The leadership overcame its sense of the sacredness of the old rules, which even in secular structures become anointed with an aura of the holy. With the support of the Academy's leadership, new procedures and policies were developed which would further the Academy's mission of training future leaders. Continuing competition for appointment to the Academy and the evident eagerness with which midshipmen approach their training attest to the effectiveness of the changes in the rules.

Roman Catholic seminaries likewise heard recommendations for change in the decrees of Vatican Council II. Unfortunately, the Purple Kingdom could not allow these profound changes to be made. The organizational pathology ran so deep that the old rules remained immutable. When resorting to Madison Avenue to advertise for manpower and characterizing those not attracted to seminaries as victims of an erotic environment, Church authorities demonstrated that they had missed a fundamental point: the rules need updating. Bishops act and sound like some of the old alumni of the Naval Academy. They both know what used to work under former conditions of service. The lesson to learn from the Academy is that while the service remains the same, the conditions have changed, and so must the rules, which means a revised organizational structure must be created. Of course, these changes are painful for those entrenched in the status quo. Lots of administrative hours went down the tubes when there ceased to be reason to police midshipmen, monitoring them for compliance with rules such as assembling on time, wearing the prescribed uniform, and marching to class in silence.

Bishops should visit the Naval Academy. The superabundance of enthusiasm and talent in the brigade is impressive. Better, all of it is directed to service for others. Why don't seminaries attract a comparable number of talented individuals dedicated to leadership and service? I think the bishops should look to themselves for an answer. Do they have the selfless openness of the Academy's leadership when it listened to recommendations from the Board of Visitors? Such a capability is hard to acquire in light of the pathology in organizations.

Before any evaluation of rules can take place, clarity of purpose is vital. What business is the Church in? Is it to preserve the organization's structure? Is it to promote love of neighbor, regardless of what happens to the organization? Is it to save souls, as we used to say before Vatican II? Clarity of purpose, like the sharpness of mission understood by all members of the Naval Academy, is glaringly lacking in Roman Catholic circles, although Vatican Council II addressed this issue when it declared that the Church served two purposes: promote service to the needs of others and celebrate the sacraments.

Before bishops can follow the example of the Naval Academy, they must first clarify the purpose and role of the Church, arrive at principles of decision-making that will further this purpose and listen to extraordinary voices, like Vatican Council II, letting old rules fall where they may. But, can they listen to voices which suggest rule changes? If they listen, will they be able to find the selflessness necessary to endorse new rules, even at the expense of turf and perks? The Naval Academy's leadership did so. Although the noisy drummer lost his job, the institution is flourishing.

—17—

The Man in the Arena

It is not the critic who counts,
not the one who points out how the strong man stumbled
or how the doer of deeds might have done them better.
The credit belongs to the man who is actually in the arena,
whose face is marred with sweat and dust and blood;
who strives valiantly.
Who errs and comes short again and again,
who knows the great enthusiasms,
the great devotions,
and spends himself in a worthy cause;
who if he wins, knows the triumph of high achievement;
and who, if he fails, at least fails while daring greatly.
His place shall never be with those cold and timid
souls who know neither victory nor defeat.

—Theodore Roosevelt

Glossary

Apostolic Delegate A church official who acts as the personal delegate of the Pope to a national hierarchy.

Archbishop The jurisdictional head of an archdiocese, also an honorary title given a bishop.

Archdiocese A territorial jurisdiction under the control of an archbishop, who may or may not be a cardinal.

Assistant Pastor The title given priests assigned by the local bishop to work in a parish under the direction of the pastor.

Baltimore Catechism A question-and-answer text designed to teach the content of Roman Catholic doctrine, so called because it was formally adopted by bishops assembled in Baltimore. Multiple editions of increasing complexity were published.

Bishop One ordained to the episcopacy, the highest level of the sacrament of Holy Order. Only one bishop in a diocese, or archdiocese, has jurisdiction of the territory; all other bishops assigned are called auxiliary bishops. They may or may not also be pastors of specific parishes.

Bridge The elevated space in the forward superstructure of a ship, whence come orders for its control.

Canon Law Initially, the code of Roman Catholic laws proclaimed in 1918. Now, the generic name for any official listing of Church rules.

Cardinal The highest honorary title conferred by the Roman Catholic Church. Current usage restricts the honor to members of the clergy, usually high-ranking officials.

Chancellor
The person in charge of the chancery.

Chancery
A place for storing Church documents. In the Roman Catholic Church of the United States, it functions also as the executive office of the local bishop.

Chaplain
An officer in the Chaplains' Corps, always also a minister, priest, or rabbi, sponsored by one of the recognized religious bodies of the United States.

Church
Meaning depends on usage:
(1) the structured organization of a particular grouping of people, sharing belief in a given set of doctrines.
(2) the collective of people who practice the Gospel message with faith in Christ, apart from organizational considerations.

Collegiality
A sharing of authority. The pope, bishops and all communities within the church assume co-responsibility for decision-making.

Conclave
A gathering of cardinals to elect a new pope.

Congregation of Christian Studies
The agency in Rome charged with seminary and educational policies.

Congregation of Seminaries
The Title of the Congregation of Christian Studies prior to Vatican II.

Cruiser
A warship of middle size between a battleship and a destroyer. During WWII, light cruisers carried six-inch guns, heavy cruisers carried eight-inch ones.

Conscience
A choice after evaluation of known facts between the moral rightness, or wrongness, of a particular action.

Council
An official assembly of Church representatives. There are several types: ecumenical, or general, which gathers representatives from the entire world; regional, which gathers representatives from a particular area or nation;

local, which gathers representatives from a diocese or specific community.

Council of Trent A solemn gathering of bishops in Trent, Italy, from 1545 to 1563 in response to the Protestant Reformation. Its decrees gave the major direction to Roman Catholicism until the time of Pope John XXIII (1958 - 1963).

Consistory A convocation of cardinals, called by the Pope, with the intention of announcing his designation of new cardinals.

Deacon The first and lowest of the ordained ranks in the Roman Catholic Church. Deacons may preach and distribute the Eucharist to the faithful.

Deposit of Faith The teachings of Jesus Christ that salvation of the human race is an accomplished fact, and that human history is evolving to the Kingdom of God, which is already at hand whenever one human responds to the need of another.

Diocese The territorial division assigned to the jurisdiction of a bishop. Generally, the population numbers less than that of an archdiocese.

Doctrine An official teaching of a church.

Dogma A doctrine which enjoys solemn promulgation by the highest authority in the Church (popes and councils). Denial of a dogma constitutes heresy.

Domestic Prelate An honorary title, the senior of two grades of monsignor. Holders wear a purple-colored cassock.

Dry Dock A space into which a ship can be moved and from which water can be pumped to allow work on the exterior below the water line.

Ecumenical A theological position which allows for the experience, doctrine and dogma of other churches.

Encyclical	A letter written by a pope and given general circulation.
Ensign	The lowest commissioned officer rank in the US Navy.
Excommunication	The expulsion of an individual from a church.
Faith	The acceptance of a proposition based on the authority of the proposer. Personal knowledge of God is based on the declarations and authority of Jesus Christ.
Freedom	The capacity to choose. It is limited by such influences as cultural conditioning, parental upbringing and limited knowledge of human nature.
General Quarters	The watch condition for battle readiness. All personnel have assigned stations and functions at which they remain for the duration of this condition.
Gospel	The good news, proclaimed by Jesus Christ, interpreted and recorded in the writings of Matthew, Mark, Luke and John: the Kingdom of God is already among us. We see it wherever one person responds to the need of another, like giving one in thirst a cup of water. Participation is open to all persons of good will.
Gregorian University	An undergraduate and graduate educational institution in Rome, Italy. It is staffed by Jesuits from around the world. Its specialty is theology. Seminarians from the North American College attend classes there.
Hell	Literally, the realm of the dead. It is the choice of one who rejects a life in community with God and neighbor. Such an individual chooses self-annihilation, or a choice for nothingness. Hence, it is neither a place nor a state of life. It is the condition of non-being.

Hierarchical	Pertaining to ecclesiastical office-holders.
Hierarchy	The ordained ministers in the Church: pope, bishops, priests and deacons.
Holy See	The juridical title of the papacy, the person of the Pope.
Humanae Vitae	Title of the 1968 letter of Pope Paul VI in which he condemned all artificial means of birth control, declaring them to be intrinsically evil.
Infallibility	Immunity from error in matters of faith and morals.
Informed Conscience	A judgment made after careful consideration of official teachings, the findings of science, writings of theologians and the Bible.
Jesuit	Shorthand name for a member of the Society of Jesus, one of the religious orders of the Roman Catholic Church. Members of religious orders live in a community style of life and take three vows of poverty, chastity and obedience. Jesuits take a fourth vow of loyalty to the Pope.
Kingdom of God	The presence of God. Lit: the reconciling power of God. It is both a process and a reality. The process is here and now in the hearts and minds of humans; the reality is that towards which the process is evolving. The giving of self for others is the process. The reality is the presence of God in mind and heart.
Limbo	The place or state for the dead who qualify for neither the beatific vision nor eternal punishment.
Love	The giving of self for the needs of another.

Mass	Lit. the Lord's Supper, the liturgical ceremony of the Roman Catholic religion, as well as others.
Midshipman	The rank assigned by the Navy to a candidate in training for a commission as an ensign. All students at the US Naval Academy are midshipmen.
Monsignor	An honorary ecclesiastical title, conferred on members of the clergy.
Mortal Sin	A conscious and fundamental decision to completely reject God.
Mustang	The term designates an officer who has come up from the ranks to commissioned status.
North American College	A seminary and graduate residence facility in Rome, Italy for students sent by bishops in the United States. Seminarians attend classes at the Gregorian University. Graduate students choose from the many Church-sponsored graduate schools.
Officer of the Deck	The duty officer with complete responsibility for operations at sea and in port, subject only to the commanding officer who may relieve him at any time.
Ordinary	The juridical title given to the head of a diocese, or archdiocese.
Ordination	The rite (laying on of hands, usually by a bishop) through which one is admitted to the diaconate, the priesthood, or the episcopate.
Original Sin	The contentious state into which all humans are born.
Plebe	The title of a first-year student at the U.S. Naval Academy.

Priest	One who has received ordination to the second Order, the one after diaconate and before episcopate.
Papal Chamberlain	The junior of the two grades of monsignor, considered part of the papal household. As such, they march in papal processions next to the Pope, wearing white fur capes over their cassocks. They wear red piping on black cassocks, in contrast to domestic prelates who wear purple cassocks. The rank is strictly honorary.
Pastor	The ordained priest assigned by the bishop to manage the spiritual and temporal needs of a geographic portion of a diocese or archdiocese. Canon law grants the pastor title to the material income therefrom as a benefice for his support. Most pastors in the United States receive a monthly stipend, over and above household maintenance.
Pope	The senior official of the Roman Catholic Church.
Pope John XXIII National Seminary	Located in Weston, Massachusetts, it offers a four-year course to the priesthood for candidates who have had prior careers in the business and professional worlds. Graduates serve in parishes of the United States, Canada and Australia.
Purgatory	The state of purification necessary after death.
Rector	The ecclesiastical superior of a residence for clergy, as in a parish staffed by members of a religious order, or in an educational institution, as in a seminary.
Reign of God	The process of activating the Kingdom of God.
Religion	The institutionalized expression of faith in God.
Roman Catholic	One who considers official Roman Catholic teaching before making a decision as to the moral rightness or wrongness of an action.

Rosary   A form of private prayer in which a bead counter is used. It is circular in shape, with five segments of ten beads, the spacing between the segments marked by a bead larger than those within the segments. The "Lord's Prayer" is recited at the larger beads and the "Hail Mary" is said at the smaller beads.

Salvation   The end product of faith, a permanent union with God and neighbor.

Schism   A breaking off from the main body by a group, usually applied to separation from unity with the Pope.

St. John's Seminary   Located in Brighton, Massachusetts, it trains candidates for ordination to the priesthood, primarily in the service of the Archdiocese of Boston.

Secular Clergy   The category of all priests ordained for the service of a specific diocese, or archdiocese; generally they are assigned to territorial parishes. They differ from priests in religious orders who live in a community with a vow of poverty, which prohibits the ownership, but not the use of property. A third category includes priests ordained on patrimony. They are not subject to service in a diocese, archdiocese, or religious community. Ordination on title of patrimony is not a practice in the United States.

Seminary   An ecclesiastically-sponsored institution for the education and training of future clergy. The Council of Trent laid down rules for Roman Catholic seminaries which continued in force until the era of Pope John XXIII.

Sin   A missing of the mark, a deliberate infidelity to the requirement to love a neighbor.

Supernatural   That which exceeds the power and capacity of human nature.

Theology   Reason reflecting on articles of faith.

**Titular Bishop,
or Archbishop**

A bishop, or archbishop, without jurisdiction over a diocese or archdiocese. They hold title to defunct and therefore honorary jurisdictions.

U.S. Naval Academy

Located in Annapolis, Maryland and sponsored by the Federal Government of the United States to develop midshipmen mentally, morally and physically, and to imbue them with the highest ideals of duty, honor and loyalty in order to provide graduates dedicated to a career of naval service with potential for future development in mind and character to assume the highest responsibilities of command, citizenship and government.

Vatican City

An independent geographic space in Italy under the civil jurisdiction of the Pope.

Vatican Council I

Held in Vatican City from 1869 to 1870. It treated matters surfaced by the Age of Enlightenment, especially reason as it relates to faith, the primacy of the papacy and infallibility.

Vatican Council II

Held in Vatican City from 1962 to 1965. It ushered in the most major developments made to doctrine and practice since the early Church opened its doors to Gentiles and did away with Jewish laws.

Vice Chancellor

The office immediately below that of chancellor.

Vice Rector

The second in command in a seminary, the person charged with student discipline and evaluation.

Wake

The time during which a deceased person is viewed by the public, prior to formal liturgical services. It is a time to offer condolences to the bereaved and say private prayers.

Ward Room

The space in a warship reserved for meals and relaxation of a ship's officers.

Watch Duty   The Navy equivalent of workplace duty in civilian life. Vital ship functions require 24-hour attention, such as engines and steering. Wartime cruising adds readiness for gunfire.

Your Eminence   The title of address proper for cardinals in the Roman Catholic Church.

Your Excellency   The title of address proper for bishops and archbishops in the Roman Catholic Church.

Your Holiness   The title of address proper for the Pope.